MONSTER
BOSS

D0292446

MONSTER BOSS

Strategies for Surviving and Excelling When Your Boss is a Nightmare

Patricia King, author of *Never Work for a Jerk*

BUSINESS

Avon, Massachusetts

Copyright © 2008 by Patricia King
All rights reserved.
This book, or parts thereof, may not be reproduced in any
form without permission from the publisher; exceptions are
made for brief excerpts used in published reviews.

Published by Adams Business, an imprint of
Adams Media, an F+W Publications Company
57 Littlefield Street, Avon, MA 02322. U.S.A.
www.adamsmedia.com

ISBN 10: 1-59869-399-9
ISBN 13: 978-1-59869-399-7

Printed in the United States of America.

J I H G F E D C B A

Library of Congress Cataloging-in-Publication Data
is available from the publisher.

This publication is designed to provide accurate and authoritative information with regard to the subject matter covered. It is sold with the
understanding that the publisher is not engaged in rendering legal,
accounting, or other professional advice. If legal advice or other expert
assistance is required, the services of a competent professional person
should be sought.

—From a *Declaration of Principles* jointly adopted by
a Committee of the American Bar Association and
a Committee of Publishers and Associations

Many of the designations used by manufacturers and sellers to distinguish their product are claimed as trademarks. Where those designations
appear in this book and Adams Media was aware of a trademark claim,
the designations have been printed with initial capital letters.

This book is available at quantity discounts for bulk purchases.
For information, please call 1-800-289-0963.

For
David, Kerry Ann, Ted,
Emma, Lillie, Alexander, and Nathaniel

In Memory of
Samuel Puglise, Beloved Father

CONTENTS

ACKNOWLEDGMENTS

Thank you to:

Kerry Ann King, who helped me develop the concept for this book.

Nancy Love, my agent and my supporter.

Mary Frances Hickey, life-long friend, marvelous editor, ever-ready morale booster.

Dr. Edward M. Steen, who provided information on substance abuse.

Laurie Berke, John Linder, Jane McIntosh, Mark Puglise, Paul Puglise, and Max Nissenholtz who contributed their stories and their wisdom.

INTRODUCTION:
WHERE COURAGE COMES FROM

According to a recent CNN report, 67 percent of people say they hate their jobs. The vast majority of unhappy workers blame their bosses. Without question, having a monster boss is one of life's challenges. No matter how bad you think it is, you have a choice: to quiver and hide or to stand up and do something.

Most likely, it scares you a bit even to think about fighting back. It might even terrify you—make you feel as you might if Frankenstein had you up over his head and was about to toss you in the lake. What can you do?

Imagine this: You can learn from the movies. The recent film of H. G. Wells's classic *War of the Worlds* is a case in point. It tells of an ordinary guy, barely able to take care of himself and his kids. Monsters come up out of the ground and wreck his neighborhood, collapse bridges, zap the electrical grid. Havoc reigns, and he must stand and fight or give up not only his own life, but those of his beloved children as well.

There he is—the classic American fictional hero—nobody extra special, a crane operator from the docks, who suddenly, because of extraordinary circumstances, must save himself and his loved ones. The monsters leave him no choice. We know he will win in the end, but that does not stop us from wanting to watch just how horribly they threaten him and his family and how strong and brave and clever he must be to defeat his monsters, despite his fear, his interim set backs, his moments of profound self-doubt. We love this stuff. And well we should. Monster movies are parables for how we must all stand up to life—not to monsters that come out of the ground to eat highway overpasses and vaporize the neighbors. But to the everyday challenges of ordinary life, like having a monster boss.

Lots of us learned in school that we can succeed with those in authority only by doing what they say and not asking any questions. Sometimes didn't it seem as if the purpose of high school was to teach us to comply with stupid requirements and perform mindless activities? But passively tolerating whatever the monsters dish out will never make you the hero of your own life.

You can do something about abusive management and not lose your job. You do not have to choose between destroying your stomach lining and providing food for your kids. This book will help you figure out what to do and how to do it, so you can earn your living without sacrificing your spirit in the process.

This is not going to be easy. Heroes never have it easy. And things are not getting any better for the badly managed. In fact, matters have gotten a lot worse since my first book on this subject, *Never Work for a Jerk*, published in 1988. Problem bosses rob employees of their job satisfaction, motivation, promotions, pay raises, and pensions. At their most dastardly, they destroy people's health—physical and mental. Unfortunately, in recent years, diminishing job growth and job outsourcing have given bullies and tyrants free reign; their employee-victims cannot easily pick up and find another job. Most people feel powerless in the face of on-the-job stress. They get up every morning with that same awful feeling: "Oh, no, do I have to go back there?" They drag themselves to the job, leaking motivation all the way. They hang on to the job they hate—without taking any positive steps to make it better—until it's too late to turn things around.

The most common reason people give for this passive acceptance of misery is fear of losing their jobs. Yet fearful behavior winds up creating exactly what they fear most. You can easily spot the dynamics. Eventually, the abused employee completely loses her motivation and then, instead of bringing all her energy and creativity to her job, she just goes through the motions, cutting corners, wasting her time thinking about how unhappy it makes her instead of focusing on how to do the work better. Not noticing the mistakes on her own desk, she grouses with her colleagues about the boss. Eventually, without the will to truly succeed, she fails, becoming another piece of dead wood in the corporate lumberyard. And then, she loses her job.

We have all seen the parade of lifeless zombies dragging themselves in to work every day, leaking motivation, leaving it in their footprints as they cross the parking lot and enter the building. Do not join the sad ranks of the living dead. This book can help you cope, but more than that, it can show you how to fix your situation, or, if you decide there is no hope, when and how to extricate yourself. It will help you survive until you can find another job and fire your current boss.

The problem of bad bosses is timeless. A book on this subject, in hieroglyphics, would have sold well among the work crews on the Great Pyramids of Giza. In the United States lately, truly dreadful bosses have been making headlines for their indictable behavior. Breathtaking greed and malfeasance among top executives has become a political issue, affecting thousands, if not millions. Many bosses seek to extract more and more work for less pay from their employees, while extracting more and more wealth for themselves, often to the detriment, if not the ruination, of the companies they run. Enron, Tyco, WorldCom: Executive criminals on parade. Grist for the mill of politicians and talk show hosts.

Monstrous management affects more than just your time spent at work. Tension on the job can make you cranky at home. It can make you physically sick. This book will help you clarify your situation, discover ways to cope, address problems head-on, and stay sane.

Using monsters as metaphors may seem humorous, but it will also help you keep your situation in perspective; a sense of humor can ameliorate stress. But do not let the breezy tone fool you. Monster bosses endanger us all, not just their employees. Their abuses weaken the companies they run and thus our country's economy. The drag they create on employee motivation cuts into productivity. Wrong-headed management can lead organizations off the financial cliff. Confused or abused employees do not produce results efficiently. Instead, they waste time conforming to useless rules, yessing their bosses, and worrying about losing their jobs. They squander time in false starts, guessing what the boss wants and completing useless tasks because they couldn't decipher what their uncommunicative boss wanted. Mindlessly pleasing the boss and then telling each other what a zoo we work in has become a national pastime. What a waste!

Instead of producing value for our society, too many of us work for people who produce only excessive and unnecessary stress. To cure this malady, we all need to take an active part in solving the problem. Collectively, we must stop this damage to our economy and to the fabric of our corporate society. Instead of lamenting, we must take action to save ourselves, our organizations, and our economy.

Before we can wage the battle, we have to diagnose the problem, then go after its causes. On a personal level, this book offers cogent and helpful advice: truly useful steps you can take, scripts to aid your communications, as well as illustrative anecdotes that will help you understand the issues and find comfort in knowing that you are not alone. If you cannot change the dynamics of your relationship with your boss, you can find ways to survive until you extricate yourself from the situation. In the process you will also learn the signs that will help you choose a better boss next time.

After a discussion of your role in the monster wars, you will find a quiz to help you figure out what kind of monster threatens you and how dangerous he is. Once you have answered the questions, you will be able to go directly to the chapter that addresses your boss. You will discover what weapons you need to defeat him. Other chapters will provide advice on how to communicate with and outsmart monster bosses. Take heart. You can learn to become the hero of your own monster movie.

1

YOU VS. MONSTER BOSS

> "I'm an expert in doormats. I'm an expert in victims.
> They were the best parts. And when I woke up—sociologically,
> politically, and creatively—I could no longer take those parts
> and look in the mirror."
> Shirley MacLaine, as quoted in *Ms.* magazine

Who would you rather play in a movie—Van Helsing, the handsome guy who drives the stake through the heart of the perpetual neck-biter, Dracula, or the little girl Frankenstein's monster tosses in the lake? Even in fictional worlds in fantasy stories on movie screens, the people who get the most love and admiration (played by the actors who get the biggest bucks, by the way) are the people who stand up for themselves and what they believe in and find a way to triumph over adversity. Your monster boss could be so scary that the very thought of switching from being his victim to becoming your own hero might intimidate you. Remember this: the more horrible the monster, the more interesting the story, and the more loved and admired the hero or heroine.

Your first step is to find the will to fight. You need to find the courage to say to yourself: "I am going to solve this problem—go over, under, around, or through it—to a point where I can make my current circumstances work for me, or

I am going to find my way out of this dark dead-end street to a place where the sun is shining."

Here's a sobering thought: There are 168 hours in a week; if you spend 40 hours working, an hour for lunch or breaks each day, an hour getting ready for work each day, and an hour each day commuting, you have only 113 hours left. If you sleep 8 hours per night, you have only 57 hours left—for buying groceries, cooking your food and eating, helping the kids with their homework, doing the laundry, exercising, and enjoying some relaxation or time with your spouse. Even with no overtime and a relatively easy commute, you are spending roughly half your weekly waking hours at work or on work-related activities. Most likely you spend more. How you spend your time at work is about half—*or more*—of how you spend your entire life!

It's vital to be realistic about your career. If you are spending more than half of your waking life on the job, you must find some important satisfactions at work or more than half of your life will be empty. You need to work to support yourself and your family, but work should be more than a source of funds. Freud defined maturity and happiness as knowing how to love and how to work. If you abdicate your responsibility for what happens to you on the job, you are giving someone else (in your case a monster) control over a significant portion of your time on this planet.

You may think that what happens to you at work is not your "real life," that what really counts happens at home, but doing so effectively shortens your "real life" by about a third. It is urgent that you take control of the huge chunk of your life that you spend at work.

You get to choose how you live your life. But you really should make an informed choice, based on your values, your capabilities, and your needs as a human being. And it is a choice you must make consciously and conscientiously. Don't let it be something you just slip into because circumstances—the luck of the draw—put you there.

Crossing the Bridge

Let's look at a scenario that mimics how you make this choice. Do you have to cross a bridge or overpass every day on your way to and from work? Imagine this: One day you leave work and start for home. Since you make this trip every day, you drive on automatic pilot, albeit aware of the traffic and conscious of the news or music on the radio. Suddenly you arrive at the bridge and find it is gone, washed away in a flash flood. You have come this far, and now your road is blocked. You sit there a moment in disbelief and frustration at the inconvenience. But after you get over the surprise, what do you do? Do you give up? Do you decide to pull over and camp out in your car until someone comes and rebuilds the bridge for you? Do you decide that you can no longer get home and that you now have to find a different place to live on this side of whatever river or chasm your bridge traversed? Of course not. You say, "Oh rats," (or Oh something) and you find another way to get home.

Home is where you have to get to, no matter what. There is no way you would just cave in and give up trying to get there. Whatever the obstacle, you will find a way to circumvent it. Even if it were to take hours, even days. Whatever the effort.

Your goal of having a job where you earn your living with your motivation, your mental and physical health, and your dignity intact is a form of finding your way home. You have the right to decent treatment, a safe work environment, a stab at career progress, and a modicum of job satisfaction. This is your bottom line. You do not give up on these expectations any more than you would give up on going home.

Bridge out. New route required. You might have to get out a road map or to punch some information into your GPS to find another way home. This book can be your GPS for finding a solution to your problems with a monster boss. There is a way. All you have to do is find the right buttons to push. This will not be easy, but if you are going to get home, you have to find an available route.

Is comparing your boss to a monster and yourself to a hero melodramatic? I do not think so. Dysfunctional, negative, abusive bosses are dangerous. They aren't likely to grow Freddy Krueger's long metal fingernails and scratch your eyes out, but they can inflict a lot of damage—even kill you. Their weapons are frustration and stress; and stress is a killer. Do you doubt that?

Can you find the courage you need to do something about your situation? However you summon that courage, this book will provide you with professional and practical encouragement. If nothing is going to give you the will to fight, then at least look for another job. Why waste your work life playing the game of "Ain't It Awful," or attending the weekly Friday lunchtime symposium where you and your friends tell each other what a rotten beast your boss is, take a Zantac, and go back to work? Do you want to play the part of the victim who is left behind in the second scene of the monster movie, the one who sits in the middle of the road, screaming, weeping, stunned and frozen in place while the action moves on and the hero triumphs.

If you cannot or will not fight, flee. Run to another job. You can meet your responsibilities to your family without surrendering your dignity or allowing some fiend to smother your hopes and ambitions. You don't need to sit still and be victimized by a person whose brain came out of a container labeled "abnormal."

Relative Disasters

Your friends, maybe even your own family, may tell you that you mustn't take any chances, that you should be grateful you have a job, and that you should not make waves. Clara Abramowitz got that very advice from her own mother.

Clara had come a long way. In her first job, she started out answering calls in the Customer Service Department of an international bank. She and her high school sweetheart, Frank, had married at eighteen and had two kids by the time they were twenty-four. They soon needed a second income to make ends meet. Once their youngest was three and their older son was in kindergarten, Clara's mom provided day-care for the kids so Clara could take the job.

Clara talents shone at the bank. Her three years of dealing with toddlers, she always said, proved a perfect training ground for knowing how to handle dissatisfied or frustrated customers. Clara was quickly promoted to supervisor, the person to whom the other operators transferred the most difficult callers. One day Paul, Clara's department head, passed her desk and overheard her telling one of the people she supervised how to handle customers who cried on the phone. Impressed with Clara's sagacity and the clear and encouraging way she instructed her staff, Paul put her in charge of training for the department. Without the benefit of higher education, but with a great work ethic, innate sensitivity, and intelligence, in just a few years, Clara was promoted to assistant manager of Customer Service. She began weekend courses at the local community college and hoped to earn her undergraduate degree in a couple of years.

Danger Looms

And then disaster struck. Clara's came in a form familiar to corporate America—a merger. The logo on the Web site remained the same, but another company took over her bank. And Paul, her boss and mentor, who had nurtured her career, was sent off to early retirement and replaced by the customer service manager of the merging bank.

Alien Invasion! This is the way it always happens in the movies. In a peaceful valley where all is right with the world—

the heroine is a nice, hard-working mom with a good family life, a helpful grandmother, a cute husband with a decent job, and couple of freckle-faced kids. And then creepy things quietly invade the valley and disturb the peace.

Shortly after the transition, Clara noticed that Gillian, her new boss, never asked her a question. Clara imagined that Gillian was just trying to establish her authority, like a teacher might do with a new class. She figured that once Gillian got to know her, things would settle down.

Losing Ground

Then Gillian took away something dear to Clara. For years, Clara had been attending the monthly Advertising and Public Relations departmental meetings, of which Customer Service was a part. Every other month, she gave a report of the major concerns bank customers voiced in their calls. Keeping track of the issues had been Clara's idea. She put the data into spreadsheets and analyzed how customers' concerns changed over time. Paul had taken Clara to the monthly meetings where she presented an oral report. Speaking in front of all those people frightened her at first, but the executive vice president had encouraged Clara by asking pertinent questions and thanking her for her ideas. She soon looked forward to participating in the meetings; being there made her feel important, in on things, as if she mattered to the larger organization.

After the invasion, Gillian instructed Clara to write the report but not to bother coming to the meeting. She said, "I know my management. They are used to really polished presentations."

When Clara turned in her report, Gillian belittled Clara's sentence structure and complained about having to rewrite the whole thing. Then she strode off to the meeting to present it as her own.

That was Clara's blackest day since Paul left.

Then, as always occurs in horror movies, the scene darkened, the music grew gloomy, and the characters in Clara's story turned menacing. Kate, one of Clara's direct reports, who had come from the other bank, asked her if it was true that she never went to college. "I am going now," Clara replied matter-of-factly.

Later that day, Clara saw Kate and Gillian laughing. She suppressed her suspicions that they were laughing at her lack of a college degree, but she was wary of the women's chumminess, and she felt left out and vulnerable.

Digging In

As best she could, Clara hid her anger and disappointment about the way Gillian treated her. At home, her husband got so angry when she complained to him that she stopped talking to him about it. His ranting against Gillian only made her feel worse. And Clara's mother urged her to swallow her pain and endure the situation. "It's only a job. You shouldn't take what those people say so seriously. They have kept you on when quite a few people lost their jobs. Let that be enough. Besides you have really gotten ahead there. It's a good job. You do not want to lose it." Clara convinced herself that she had to keep the job for the sake of her kids.

Not long afterward, Clara ran into Paul, her former boss and guru, on the college campus and couldn't resist asking his advice. Paul shook his head while she was telling her the story. "Get out of there," he said simply. "That's what I'd do."

But Clara couldn't bring herself to leave the job. She kept thinking back to what her subordinate Kate, had pointed out—that Clara had no college degree. She was going to school now, but just on weekends, and it would be years before she could earn a degree. How would she find another management job without a college degree?

So she put on her mask of professionalism every day when she arrived at work. She lowered her profile, her sights, and her hopes. After a while, work made her so tired that she didn't have the energy to keep going to school. She watched Gillian move up in the organization and her subordinate Kate get promoted into another department, and through a series of reorganizations, Kate eventually became Clara's boss. Clara still excelled at her job, but the only time she enjoyed it was when she stepped in to deal with particularly difficult customers—no one handled those situations better than she did.

The alien invaders did not kill Clara, but they enslaved her. They decided what role Clara would play, and they kept her in "her place." They figured out how to make her feel inferior and how to feed off her work. They turned Clara into a zombie. They put her in the cellar, and she dutifully stayed there—she let them do it.

What a waste. All that enthusiasm and creativity zapped out of existence.

Escaping the Trap

Hiding in the cellar to escape the monster may work, but you wind up spending the rest of your life in the basement!

If your boss behaves like a monster and has already bitten off a piece of what you used to be, and you are not in a position to fight and win, get out. I mean O-U-T. Becoming a zombie is not a way to save your life. Instead, plan your exit and escape, even if you have to do it slowly and carefully. We'll discuss escape plans in the coming chapters. For now, understand that as soon as you create a plan, the stress will lessen. You can withstand a certain amount of suffering as long as you know it is going to end—soon.

If you decide to stay where you are, then you need to try to improve your situation. If you cannot change things, at the very least, you need a better way to cope. If you are convinced that your best course of action is to stay, then you need to find a way to accept the situation, to grin and bear it. But you have to grin while you are bearing it. If you constantly rail against your monster while passively enduring him, everyone you know will get sick and tired of listening to you complain. Learn to laugh at it. See the monster's ego, and your own, for what they are. Stop letting anger and frustration cripple you. Use the time you have away from the job to get pleasures and satisfactions from life. Do your job well and leave the frustration behind when you leave for home.

Find Allies

One thing that can help a great deal in dealing with a monster is allies. Not just people who will commiserate with you, not just the people in your department who are your fellow victims, but someone who believes in you and will encourage you to realize your potential. Not just a sympathizer. You need a cheerleader, an ego booster. A sage supporter who has the courage to tell you when your thinking is off base, but also someone with a positive attitude toward you as a person. If you have a mentor or a friend who can truly help you over the difficult times, help you keep your grievances in perspective, and rejoice with you when you triumph, you will know where to go for the advice and the encouragement that will motivate you to solve this problem.

Even when things are going well, a number of bad things can happen. You could be fired or demoted. You could get stuck in a crummy job. When you suffer a setback, you need a way to hold on to your sanity. Knowing how to cope with adversity is part of knowing how to survive on this planet. The best thing to do in a bad situation is learn from it. That learning will inform your future. Besides, learning is one of the two or three noble things you will do in your life. Do as much of it as you can. Some people think it is why you are here in the first place. A supportive mentor will help make that learning happen and transform disaster into a positive force in your life.

Unless you learn to handle unpleasant situations and to take steps to right them, you will likely succumb to stress. Heart attacks, depression, insomnia, and a ruined family life lay in wait for you. Who wants that? Use this book to find a way to fight your demons.

The first thing you do is arm yourself; but how?

Set Goals

There is a moment in every scary movie where you see determination in the hero's eyes. The shock and denial phase is over, the running about and screaming and shouting has gotten his blood pumping and his adrenalin levels focused at last. Something has shifted within our hero, and we know that now we are going to see action, not running away. The hero fights. She thinks in clever, creative ways. She begins to use whatever she has handy—the hairspray in the medicine cabinet, the gas in her car. Weapons that have been lying around unused are now grasped and brought to bear. This is it, folks. This is where the fun begins.

Are you there? If you are reading this book, you must be close. You are looking for an answer. You are at the tipping point. Take heart, you *are* going to do this. You may feel discouraged along the way, but you will not be deterred. If your first efforts don't work, you will keep trying new things until something gives. You will be a person who works at it until it works for you.

To do this, you need to set goals. Stop for a minute now and think what those objectives ought to be. You choose. Turn to Appendix A at the back of this book, to the page labeled "Goals." Get a pen or open a document on your computer.

Describe how you want things to be—with your relationship with your boss, what you want from your job in terms of compensation, satisfaction, time off, respect, whatever you most desire. Even if your goal doesn't feel fully formulated, make a stab at this. It doesn't have to be perfect. If you don't get it right the first time, you can always change it.

The hardest part of getting what you want is to decide what it is you want. It is scary to confront your own goals and commit yourself to them. If you fail, you might feel worse than you already do. The monster called failure is scarier than a werewolf with tentacles that emit poison slime. If you let yourself set a goal and then you cannot achieve it, it will kill you, right? Not really. Consider this person:

- At the age of twenty-three, he lost his job.
- He ran for state legislature and was defeated.
- The following year, he started a business, which failed.
- Two years later, his sweetheart died.
- The following year, he had a nervous breakdown. (Do you blame him?)
- Two years after that, he was defeated for Speaker of his state legislature.
- Five years later, he was defeated in his bid for the nomination to the U.S. Congress.
- Five years after that, having been elected to Congress, he lost renomination.
- The following year, he tried to get a job as a land officer but was rejected.
- Five years later, he lost the election for U.S. senator.
- Two years later he lost his bid to become the vice presidential candidate.
- Two years after that, he was again defeated in his run for the U.S. Senate.
- Two years later, he was elected president of the United States.

He was Abraham Lincoln.

Many, many highly successful people have credited their failures with teaching them all they needed to know so that success did not elude them forever. So, can you take the plunge and commit yourself to a goal?

Talking about how failure will not kill you is not to say that failure is inevitable. You can reduce its likelihood by setting achievable goals. Aim for what you can achieve, but also stretch a bit. If you make your goal too easy, there will be no real reward in achieving it. It will bore you. Even a small effort put in trying to reach it will not seem worth it because the reward will be so paltry. On the other hand, don't get so overly ambitious that you will feel daunted and give up before you start.

The trick here will be to assess what's possible with the monster in the corner office. You need to be realistic about who he is and what you can achieve with him.

Dealing in the art of the possible is critical. It was for Linda Arnaud, for example, when she worked for Chip. She calls him a boy's boy. He loved being one of the guys. He was the CEO, and he kept all his male direct reports close. They went out together to drink and smoke cigars. They were the medieval knights of the roundtable, excluding women from their circle. They had mores and customs as arcane as those in a court of ancient England. Chip demanded a high degree of loyalty, and he got it. He maintained a strict pecking order among his followers, and they obeyed it. They knew their tribal obligations. They knew that if they were Chip's, he would take care of them—over whole careers, whole lifetimes. A cult of mutual loyalty.

This was and is Wall Street. Linda is brilliant at what they actually do there. When she starts talking about EBITDA or IBT or the futures of derivatives, her friends smile and nod as if they understand her and hope there will not be a quiz later.

Chip talked to her about that technical stuff with great enthusiasm and ease, but with the people who were the real insiders in the company he talked other stuff—golf, squash, shooting. They actually went out and did these things together. Linda was never included. She tried to be. She learned golf and got pretty good at it. She talked about it with them at lunches where she could not be excluded. They smiled indulgently and talked about fly-fishing. It became clear to her that the art of the possible did not include her becoming one of them.

"What I really wanted," she told me, "was a place at the table." But she slowly realized that she was never going to get it. Her friend Annamarie suggested a lawsuit for discrimination against women. Linda saw the justice in that, but she also saw years of legal hassles and churning in her gut. She decided not to sue Chip for making her feel excluded. She focused on a goal that made much more sense. A place at the table would have been nice, but she went for a shot at making as much money as the male players.

She went to Chip, who was no dope after all, despite his dopey attitudes, looked at him steadily and evenly and told him it was time for her to call on clients on her own and to get commissioned on consulting projects she brought in and managed.

At first Chip acted as if her request was a joke. "I am serious," she repeated with her biggest, brightest smile. "Tell me you will consider it." His bushy eyebrows met. His-good-old boy expression turned almost grave. She could tell it was dawning on him: she wasn't going to give up. He didn't say yes, but he didn't say no, either. He sees, she thought, that under my sweet face and understanding smile there lurks a pain in the butt. Linda added a few watts to her smile, and said, "I'll tell you what. Watch the results from the Bing and Masters project? It's almost completed. As it winds down, and I am ready for a new assignment, you can decide."

He actually stood up at that moment, and that's when she knew she was going to get what she wanted. He never stood up at one-to-one meetings unless he had reached some important decision. Later on she worried. Maybe that important decision had been to fire her, to sabotage her current project, to find some nefarious way of ruining her career—give her a project that was near impossible and set her up to fail. There were moments when she felt so scared she regretted having stood up to him. But she comforted herself with the thought that the reward would be worth the risk.

When her project ended, she asked for another meeting. She was very soft about it, almost apologetic. Forcefulness might have worked with someone else, but not with Chip—not from her, not from anyone. His boys were all brilliant, but none would ever challenge him overtly. Knights of the Roundtable must never do that.

"I have already decided to give you a shot at a project," he said.

Just to be sure she asked, "Is it an easy one or a hard one?"

"Moderate," he said. "You will not have any real problem with it."

She suppressed any feelings of triumph, put her hand over her heart, and bowed her head slightly—just as she has seen an actress playing Maid Marian do in an old Robin Hood movie. "Thank you so much," she said.

What made Linda successful was her insight. She could have blundered, but she didn't. She studied Chip and knew what would work with him.

That's what you need to do. Having set your goals, you need to consider what is achievable with your monster boss. Then you will be able to make informed choices and arm yourself with the weapons that will help you achieve those goals.

Wooden stakes through the heart, wolf bane, garlic, bacteria fatal to aliens, a glass of water that can dissolve a witch—what do you need to defeat your monster? First you need to figure out what kind of monster you have. Turn the page and find out.

2

MONSTER BOSS QUIZ

"... a monster of so frightful mien as to be hated needs but to be seen."

Alexander Pope, "An Essay on Man"

So your boss is a monster. Okay. But what kind? This makes a difference. What you require to defeat the beast depends on whether he emits poison gas or zaps people with laser rays. Do you need a figurative stake to drive through her heart (presuming she even has one)? Or do you just need to find a place to hide while the bacteria on the planet quietly destroy him?

This quiz will help you isolate what kind of a monster boss you have and allow you to go directly to the chapters most useful to you. The quiz score will also tell you how dangerous your monster is.

A note: Bosses—good and bad—can be male or female, so we will use the pronouns "he" and "she" interchangeably. There is no implication here that a man or a woman is more or less likely to be one type of monster or another. They all come in all shapes—and some of the worst seem quite attractive and benign at first look . . . but more about that later. Right now, let's ID this critter.

Answer the questions honestly. Here goes: 0 = Always, 1 = Almost Always, 2 = Sometimes, 3 = Almost Never, 4 = Never

SECTION A

0 1 2 3 4   Is your boss firmly committed to what he does?

0 1 2 3 4   Does he spend time on important work and avoid trivia?

0 1 2 3 4   Is your boss confident in herself?

0 1 2 3 4   Does she know how to win battles?

0 1 2 3 4   Does he learn from his own mistakes?

0 1 2 3 4   Can your boss get tough when it's really necessary?

SECTION B

0 1 2 3 4   Do you report to or get work from only one person? (If your answer is 0, skip the rest of this section.)

0 1 2 3 4   Do your bosses talk to one another and coordinate the priorities for work they assign to you?

0 1 2 3 4   When they assign you tasks, do they ask you about your workload?

0 1 2 3 4   Do they avoid using you as part of their competitive games?

0 1 2 3 4   Do they all participate in formal evaluations of your performance?

0 1 2 3 4   Do the people you work for generally agree on how good you are at your job?

SECTION C

0 1 2 3 4   Does your boss give you challenging assignments that help you expand your capabilities?

0 1 2 3 4   Does your boss give you the credit and recognition you deserve?

0 1 2 3 4   Does your boss make you feel like an important member of the team?

0 1 2 3 4 Does your boss consider your point of view when she makes decisions that affect you?

0 1 2 3 4 Does your boss encourage you to use your own skills and creativity?

0 1 2 3 4 Does your boss avoid win-lose battles with you?

SECTION D

0 1 2 3 4 Does your boss conduct business in an ethical, moral, and legal fashion?

0 1 2 3 4 Does she create a mutually supportive atmosphere among her subordinates?

0 1 2 3 4 Does she empathize with your position when something goes wrong?

0 1 2 3 4 Does he allow you to follow your conscience when moral judgments are called for at work?

0 1 2 3 4 Does your boss praise your good work more than she criticizes your mistakes?

0 1 2 3 4 Does she understand when personal issues impinge on your life?

SECTION E

0 1 2 3 4 Geography: Circle 4 if your boss is on another continent; 3 if he is in another country on the same continent; 2 if in another state or province; 1 if in another city; 0 if in the same office or complex.

0 1 2 3 4 How often are you and your boss in the same room?

0 1 2 3 4 Do you have a chance to talk to or e-mail back and forth with your boss at least once a day?

0 1 2 3 4 Can you get to your boss for answers to important questions within a reasonable amount of time?

0 1 2 3 4 Is your boss around to give you encouragement?

0 1 2 3 4 Does she have time for you?

SECTION F

0 1 2 3 4 Does your boss set reasonable deadlines?

0 1 2 3 4 Does your boss demand only reasonable amounts of overtime?

0 1 2 3 4 Does she make sure you have what you need to get the job done?

0 1 2 3 4 Does he staff adequately for the amount of work?

0 1 2 3 4 Does he make sure you are rewarded for your contribution?

0 1 2 3 4 Does she require you to make only reasonable demands on others—your subordinates or suppliers?

SECTION G

0 1 2 3 4 Does your boss set priorities and stick to them?

0 1 2 3 4 Is he fair in making decisions about salary, promotions, and bonuses?

0 1 2 3 4 Is your boss credible and trustworthy?

0 1 2 3 4 Is he consistent in the way he handles his job?

0 1 2 3 4 Is he even tempered?

0 1 2 3 4 Is she evenhanded in the way she treats the people who work for her?

SECTION H

0 1 2 3 4 Does your boss give you clear directions as to what he wants done?

0 1 2 3 4 Does she teach you things?

0 1 2 3 4 Does he tell you the truth about your work even if it is unpleasant?

0 1 2 3 4 Does he correct your coworkers if they need it?

0 1 2 3 4 Does she clue you in on things?

0 1 2 3 4 Does your boss communicate clearly?

SECTION I

(Note numbers in the section are reversed. 4 = Always, 3 = Almost Always, 2 = Sometimes, 1 = Almost Never, 0 = Never)

4 3 2 1 0 Does your boss touch your body inappropriately?

4 3 2 1 0 Does your boss try to seduce you?

4 3 2 1 0 Does she ask you inappropriate questions about your sex life?

4 3 2 1 0 Does she tell off-color jokes or stories?

4 3 2 1 0 Does he suggest that your advancement is tied to your sexual favors?

4 3 2 1 0 Does he display or show you sexually explicit materials and/ or use sexually degrading words to describe people?

SECTION J

(Note: Back to the original numbering system.)

0 1 2 3 4 Does your boss allow you to work independently, without an undue amount of oversight?

0 1 2 3 4 Does she require only a reasonable amount of reporting on your work?

0 1 2 3 4 Does she avoid getting mired in minutiae?

0 1 2 3 4 Does he let you make the decisions you are capable of making on your own?

0 1 2 3 4 Does he avoid correcting your inconsequential mistakes?

0 1 2 3 4 Does she let you decide how you are going to achieve your objectives, give you authority to match your responsibilities?

SECTION K

0 1 2 3 4 Does he put the needs of the organization before his own needs for power and wealth?

0 1 2 3 4 Do the people who run your company think about its long-term future?

0 1 2 3 4 Are the goals and efforts of the company management aimed at providing an excellent product or service?

0 1 2 3 4 Do the policies and practices of your company comply with the highest ethical standards?

0 1 2 3 4 Do the top executives keep their perks and compensation in line with what's reasonable?

0 1 2 3 4 Do the accounting practices of the firm follow generally accepted rules?

SECTION L

0 1 2 3 4 Can you tolerate your boss's flaws?

0 1 2 3 4 Think of all the bosses you have had: how often have they been good bosses?

0 1 2 3 4 How often in your life have you had a boss who really understood you?

0 1 2 3 4 Is emotional support or personal gratification more important to you on the job than earning a living?

0 1 2 3 4 Do you get personal satisfaction from activities away from work as well as on the job?

0 1 2 3 4 How often in your life have you found yourself in a great relationship with an authority figure?

Okay. Add up your boss's ratings in each section and enter the scores:

A		E		I		L	
B		F		J			
C		G		K			
D		H		Total			

Save L for now. It has a special significance that I will tell you about later.

Now you have got a little analysis to do. First, let's take a look at how bad a boss you have. Locate the Total score below.

SCORE	CONCLUSION
264–198	**YOUR BOSS IS TOTALLY TOXIC.** You are in grave danger of getting eaten alive on this job. Start writing your resume. Depending on the state of your health and your pocketbook, it might be wise to resign immediately. Read this book for advice on how to cope in the meantime or how to choose better next time.
197–132	**BE VERY CAREFUL.** You are in a dark alley with a person who could turn out to be a werewolf. If your boss's score is near the top of this range, the full moon is rising. It is urgent that you plan your coping strategy NOW! Read on to interpret your monster's behavior.
131–66	**THERE'S REAL HOPE.** If you can learn to avoid the sharp parts of this monster, you can probably learn to work comfortably with him. Start taking an active role in solving the problems. Follow the advice in the relevant chapters. See below to determine which ones will help you most.
65–0	**YOU HAVE A GOOD, MAYBE EVEN A GREAT BOSS.** Capitalize on her strengths and learn all you can. Read this book to find out how to make the most of your advantageous position.

Three Important Caveats

Section I: If the score for this section is higher than a 2, you have a monster for sure. Read Chapter 13 right away.

Section K: If the score for this chapter is higher than 12, even if your overall score for your boss is not bad, you may still have a BIG Monster to slay—a building-sized beast that can eat your pension plan and whose blood, if he bleeds, could permanently stain your resume. You are probably working for a Cujo Corporation. Keep going with this analysis and then read Chapter 15 first.

Section L: If your score for Section L is over 18, read Chapter 16 first. And then go on to the other chapters. You need to work on two things at once—your own perhaps unrealistic expectations *and* your beastly boss's bad behavior.

Now, circle the two or three sections where you had the highest scores on the list below and see what monster movie you are living in. The chart below also gives the location in this book of the information that will best advise you on how to slay the beast inside your boss.

SECTION WITH HIGH SCORE	GO TO THIS CHAPTER		
A	Blob Boss	Chapter 5	page 59
B	Frankenstein	Chapter 6	page 71
C	Bigfoot	Chapter 7	page 81
D	Abominable Snowman	Chapter 8	page 95
E	Loch Ness Monster	Chapter 9	page 113
F	Dracula	Chapter 10	page 131
G	Dr. Jekyll and Mr. Hyde	Chapter 11	page 143
H	The Mummy	Chapter 12	page 157
I	The Giant Squid	Chapter 13	page 165
J	Argus	Chapter 14	page 173
K	Cujo	Chapter 15	page 183
L	The Blair Witch	Chapter 16	page 193

So now you know.

By the way, really dangerous monsters can be hybrids. For instance, if she scores 21 in Section H and 20 in Section A, she is a MummyBlob. Or, your monster boss could be a BigfootCujo or an Abominable Snowman with Argus tendencies. These would be bad, very bad.

But before you get to the specifics of monster control, let's talk about the general arsenal of antimonster material that you will need to take to war. The skill you need is to communicate properly. Chapter 3 will help you develop it.

3

HOW TO SPEAK MONSTER

"UGH. ARUGH. GRRRRRUG GRRRRRUG!"
King Kong

In one of Kurt Vonnegut's marvelous short stories, a Tralfamadoran, a creature from outer space, comes to earth with
only benign intentions. He looks like a typical American
man. Nothing that you would notice about him would make
you suspicious of him. Unfortunately, however, he comes
from a planet where people communicate by farting and tap
dancing. He goes up to a suburban house, rings the doorbell
and tries to get help from the people inside. You can imagine
the results.

   To talk to your monster, you must speak to him in his
language. For some of you, this may be complicated by the
fact that you and the person you work for are not fluent in
the same language. I once watched an Italian shopkeeper
and a Japanese visitor try to complete a simple transaction
in the only language they had in common—English. The
tourist was trying to say "three," but with his accent, it came
out sounding more like "free." When the shopkeeper, with

his Italian accent, used the same word, it came out as "tree." For one not directly involved, what went on between them was almost as much fun to watch as Kurt Vonnegut's Tralfamadoran story. For merchant and tourist, though, it was painful and frustrating. They were unable to complete their transaction until a person bilingual in English and Italian intervened to lend a hand.

Speak Your Boss's Language

Conflicting mother tongues can be the problem. But there are other more insidious issues about messages, often more fraught with dangers. Communication can become impossibly garbled when two people with vastly different points of view—and goals—enter into a conversation with the confidence that they are speaking a common language. If your minds are moving in opposite directions, your words are not going to mean the same things to him as to you. Since you are the one who is trying to change the boss's mind, you are the one who has to find the proper way to proceed. To change anyone's mind about anything, you have to start from where her mind is—how she perceives problems and your roles.

Understand Your Boss's Perspective

Imagine that you are sitting in a dark corner and that there is a lamp on the other side of the room. You want to move a lamp from that side of the room to where you are sitting. If that is your objective, the task is simple. You go to the lamp, unplug it from its socket, grasp it gently but firmly, carry it to where you want it, and plug it in. Then you can turn it on and light up your corner of the room.

In other words, you have to go to where your boss's mind is on the subject in question, disconnect it from where it is now tethered, and gently but firmly move it to where you want it to be. The first step in changing anyone's mind is to figure out where that mind is now lodged. Do not try to rip the plug out of the socket. You can get hurt doing that. Proceed gently, but firmly.

Sometimes the best approach is to ask questions. "Tell me what you think we should be emphasizing in this report." "What do you think is upper management's goal for this product redesign?" "Who do you think might be the best people to work on this?" Then you can gently and respectfully suggest other ways to think about the question—couched in provisional terms. "Do you think we might also want to emphasize the customer satisfaction aspects?" "Do you suppose management might also be contemplating marketing this product to families as well as schools? If so, we should think about consumer appeal when we design the packaging." "Have you considered maybe putting Andrea and Yaki on the team, instead of Hal and Julie? Hal and Julie are pretty swamped. Andrea is almost finished with the annual survey and Yaki is a whiz at desktop publisher."

You see the tone here. You are finding a respectful way to ask, "Where is your head?" and then "Have you thought about bringing it over here?"

Know What Your Boss Really Wants

If you cannot question the boss directly, you may have to infer where her head is by understanding where she usually keeps it. Say you want her to change the priorities for two of your projects. If she always puts the cost accounting projects first because she is obsessed with costs, show her that it will cost less, take less time, and use fewer resources in the long run if you do it your way. If all she worries about is how she looks to her boss, show her how she can impress her boss by doing it your way. If you do not know what makes your boss tick, what motivates him, you cannot move him. Find out his goals and talk about them, rather than yours.

Often it is the corporate culture that prevents us from having the courage to speak up. In many companies, hardly anyone has the guts to speak directly, especially if it means disagreeing with someone in authority. Managers make vague suggestions, and in their desire to please, employees interpret the suggestions as directives. At a meeting in one of the world's largest banks, the general auditor remarked to his direct reports, "It would be interesting to know how people learn to breach computer security. I mean, can you go to school for this?" Based on the boss's expression of "interest," his assistant manager formed a task force to study the question. The members of the study group went online to research, interviewed a couple of professors, and asked their contacts at Microsoft and IBM to weigh in on the subject. Two weeks later, a thirty-page report that the general auditor really did not want showed up in his inbox.

Later we found that all six people in the Auditing Department who worked on the study thought it was an asinine waste of time for them to spend two weeks studying a moot question. They all thought the same thing—even if they identified exactly how hackers learn their skills, what could the bank do about it anyway? But they were all good corporate citizens; none of them had the nerve to disagree openly. One said she discussed the insanity of the project at lunch with her colleague, but they agreed that it would not be smart to bring up their objections.

Eventually, when the general auditor received the report, he was shocked at the time and effort that went into complying with a request he never meant to make. What he had expressed as idle curiosity his assistant manager had mistaken for a work assignment.

Give Your Boss What Will Satisfy Her

If every one of your sentences begins with I, you are generally in trouble. Your sentences should start with "you," as in, "Your goals usually center on efficiency. There may be a way to get these two projects done with less investment of time and energy."

If your monster is looking for food, feed it something besides your own head. Some creatures are *datavores*—a big meal of charts and graphs often satisfies them. Serve up a few pie charts for dessert and you can put them in a splendid mood.

There are many critters out there, especially among top-level managers who can take in nourishment only through their egos. If she responds to flattery, spread it on. Try a thin layer and see how thick you can go before she gags on it.

Listen to his rationales for what he wants to do. Whenever you can, use those same rationales to get him to make the decisions you want him to make. If he says, "We do not want to rock the boat," all the time, you can be sure he doesn't want to do anything to attract upper management's attention to himself or his group. If this is the case, you have to find a way to make what you want seem like business as usual. Offer precedents—remind him of times in the past where the same thing or nearly the same thing was done with success.

Watch his facial expressions. What he says and how he feels may be two different things. If he says he understands, and his eyes look doubtful, he may know what you are saying but not agree with it at all. If she starts to look at her fingernails, you have lost her. Learn the topics that make her pay attention.

Clarity and tact are your allies. Tact is not just a courtesy; it is a tactic. You can use it to get people to listen to you. Also brevity. Get to the point quickly. Speak softly and rationally. These are ways to keep other people's ears and minds open to what you have to say.

Have a Plan

Never, never approach a wild beast with a problem and no solution. Being told about problems without being offered solutions disturbs most bosses. It absolutely enrages the fiendish. If you are the one closest to the werewolf when the first ray of moonlight strikes its head, you are the one who will be ravaged. You may be trying to enlighten him, but do it with the daylight of solutions.

When you enter the fiend's lair to convince him to give you what you want, go in with a plan for how you will cope with contingencies. Know ahead of time how you will react if she immediately agrees. Will you ask for something more? What will you say if she says, "I haven't got time for this." How about saying: "I appreciate that you are busy right now. When can we meet to talk about this?" Be sympathetic to her schedule, but press for a day and time. If he tries to bite your head off, how about smiling broadly and saying firmly, but quietly: "If this is not the best time to talk, when can we meet?" If he says, "Never," take him at his word. Find another way to your goal or, better yet, find another job.

Start Slow

Once you are communicating, begin with small requests about easy things. Little by little your boss will begin to see meetings with you as brief, productive encounters. Then he will not anticipate trouble. A monster who thinks he is on safe ground will not pounce on the first thing that makes a noise.

If dealing with this monster inspires you to hone your communications skills, more power to you. Being able to get your points across and persuade other people will help you throughout your career. A study by the Carnegie Institute of Technology showed that interpersonal skills account for fully 85 percent of career success. Only 15 percent of your financial and work advancement depends on your technical competence. You have spent lots of time and money garnering the technical knowledge that you need to do your job. If you lack the abilities to persuade and influence through your communications, no matter how technically competent you are, you will lose out.

Be Clear

Only you can get your point of view across. Your boss cannot read your mind. Even if she tries, she may read it wrong. If you try hiding your dissatisfaction, you will unintentionally broadcast that something is eating you. The sour look on your face, your skimpy job performance, or your bickering and snide remarks will betray you. Most bosses will interpret such behavior as *your* personality problem, *your* lack of job motivation stemming from *your* personal difficulties, *your* lack of a work ethic, and definitely *your* lack of potential. To avoid sending these unintentional messages, you need to send clear, intentional ones through planned conversation.

Holding in your complaints can be dangerous in other ways, too. It will drain your energy. Keeping your mouth shut can take more out of you than speaking up. Procrastinating about these discussions almost inevitably makes them more difficult. A minor issue that would have been easy to discuss calmly can become a major source of pain. If you put it off until you cannot stand it, your emotions may get so exaggerated that you cannot come across as a rational person.

Be Calm

Overly emotional outbursts will get you a reputation as a hothead. No one, least of all your manager, will want to listen to hysterical complaints. There is often only a thin line between courage and craziness. From a distance, it may be hard to tell which side you are on. Do not go to battle over trivialities, and do not let your emotions run away with you.

Some people save up their little hurts like "award points." If you insult them by not remembering their birthday, they deposit a few points in your account. If you walk by them without saying "good morning," they put in a few more points. If you forget to copy them on an important e-mail, they score a few more. Then, when they have amassed a few thousand, they cash them all in at once, in an explosion of accusations and a tirade over old wounds.

If you take this approach, you will end up overwrought. You will come across as a person so mired in trivia, so outraged by petty issues that you cannot concentrate on the larger problems of life or work. It may seem silly to "have a talk" because someone did not invite you to a lunch, but it is better, if it really bothers you, to bring it up as a minor issue and resolve it. Your other choice is to forget it. But really forget it—for good. If you save it up, you are probably in for a shouting match with the boss just before you quit, or worse yet, as he is in the process of firing you. Know yourself; if you cannot forget it, talk about it before it becomes a thorn that festers.

Besides, letting a situation become overly emotional will negatively affect your health. Losing your temper will increase your stress and decrease your credibility.

Outbursts on your part will effectively arm a monster boss. He will use your "unreasonable" behavior against you. If you are already so outraged by the boss's misdeeds, give yourself a chance to cool off before you approach her. During the cooling-off period, redirect your riled emotions and use the energy to set your objectives, decide what you want to accomplish and why, and plan your strategy. This will help you keep your anger from getting in the way.

Be Clever

Lots of people tell themselves that they are keeping quiet because it is polite and respectful. This is another place where corporate cultures can collude with our own fears and make it hard for us to say what needs to be said to solve a problem. In some companies there seems to be an unwritten rule against saying anything negative. Someone suggests a totally harebrained scheme and no wants to point out its flaws. It would not be a good idea to shout "Are you nuts?" at most business meetings. But often people are so polite, so reluctant to question another—especially if it is the boss— that they water down their thoughts. Instead of asking the hard questions, they say things like, "That could be interesting." There are polite ways of challenging the idea without challenging the person or her authority. You can begin by saying: "Let's think about that." Follow with a question, such as: "How will the change in schedule affect the billing cycle?" You can be polite without being a patsy.

A frontal attack on an 800-pound gorilla is never a good idea. Confrontational tactics have no place in this war. You need to be direct and clear, but you must not be offensive. This applies no matter how offensive your monster has been to you. He will not listen if your ideas come at him like lobbed grenades. Try to open his mind, no matter how puny you think it is.

Be Positive

Look for common ground. If your boss is an obnoxious slob or a neurotic perfectionist, you may be so distracted by your differences that you ignore the goals you have in common. Remember that you are looking for agreement. You need to start with what you already agree on and negotiate on the basis of mutual gain.

Looking for agreements will allow you to present your-self—and your ideas—in the most attractive way. Keep your attitude positive. If you assume that everything the boss does and says is poisonous, you poison your own chances with your negative presentation. Begin by thinking that both you and the boss can win. If you don't have a glimmer of optimism left, it may be too late to save this relationship. In that case, talking things over with the boss may be just a formality. It will definitely be an exercise in frustration. Hopeless is hope-less. But if you have hope that things can improve, keep that optimistic picture in mind.

Avoid Arrogance

Never walk into that monster-occupied corner office with a look on your face that says that you know better than the boss. This is an easy mistake to make. You probably do know more. But you also have to know enough to hide that, to come across as knowledgeable, but respectful. The ability to adjust your approach to fit the situation will aid your survival in monster territory.

Mike Geary figured this out for himself. He grew up in a working class neighborhood in the Bronx. His father worked in construction, and his mother worked behind the counter at a bakery. There were a lot of kids in his family. Through sheer determination, Mike made it through Fordham Uni-versity on a scholarship and by working nights at a full-time job washing cars for a car rental agency. He dreamed of Wall Street, and when he graduated he got a position in a big financial firm.

Mike was astute, gifted at corporate deal making. He saw straight through the BS in any situation and read people bet-ter than anyone in the firm, even when he was new on the job. But once he moved up a couple of rungs on the ladder, once "his head got above water," as he described it, everyone saw he lacked the polish of all those Ivy League types and Wharton graduates who populated the firm. Confident that Mike's natural abilities could benefit the company, his department head had the vision to hire a consultant to do a Pygmalion makeover on Mike—to polish Mike's comportment so he could move with grace and ease in the circles where his abilities would lead. "I have all the steak, but I am never going to make it unless I have the sizzle," Mike told the person hired to spruce him up.

He drank in the information the executive coach gave him—how to speak without an accent; how to make a reservation in a swanky restaurant, order, and pay the bill with aplomb; theater; concerts; manners; dress. Before you knew it, he sounded, looked, and acted every inch Park Avenue. Then Mike went the whole process one better. "I signed up for an acting class," he told his executive coach.

"Tell me about this,'" she said.

"I think it's important for me to be able to express myself in a lot of different ways," Mike explained. "If I am in a meeting and I want to ask, 'Are you sure this is best for the firm? I could say that a number of ways: '*Are* you sure this is best for the firm?' Or 'Are *you* sure this is best for the firm?' Or 'Are you *sure* this is best for the firm?'

"A lot could hang on how I express myself. I want to have all the possibilities at my finger tips."

Mike took acting lessons and learned, not only how to express ideas in various ways, but how to react to what other people said so that he elicited the responses he wanted. He learned to reveal only what he intended. "Learning to act is helping me win at poker as well as at work," he said.

Eventually, Mike headed up a group negotiating deals on a nationwide basis. He also earned an MBA. His CEO reassured him that he didn't need one, but Mike was after something more than he was getting. He measured his life with a different yardstick than how much money he made and what labels his clothing carried. While at university, he became hooked on education. Eventually he moved "uptown from Wall Street," as he described it, to a professorship and eventually to dean of the business school. Everywhere he went, Mike attributed 70 percent of his success to his ability to handle people.

Focus your career hopes on your ability to understand, communicate with, and persuade others, especially your boss, and you will do well. Of course, brilliant communications strategies won't matter if your monster has fangs, tentacles, and eyes that emit deadly laser rays, but no ears. Your monster may be incapable of hearing, or she may not be able to change anything even if she sympathizes. Some contemporary corporate cultures prevent bosses from doing what is right, even if they have that rare impulse to do so.

Know Your Corporate Climate

Companies trying to figure out how to compete in the global marketplace are focusing on younger, rather than more experienced, people. Rather than mutual loyalty between the company and the employee, they focus on contract employment and short-term gains. If what you want from your job is long-term satisfaction and lifetime employment, it may not be available to you where you work. You are in the wrong place if your company is off-shoring work and replacing the old salary administration system with big bonuses tied to quarterly results.

Likewise, there is no point in asking for a raise at low-end retailers. The cheapo retail companies are focused on lowering prices to attract the maximum in sales and to make their owners—*not you*—rich. If more money is what you want, you will not find it in such a place. If you are asking for the impossible, you are not going to get it no matter how silver tongued you can make yourself.

Communication Strategies

On the other hand, there are specific techniques that will vastly increase your chances of getting what you realistically want, even if it is a stretch for your boss.

Be Timely

Time your approach. Choose the moment when your boss has the time and the mental and psychological energy to listen. If she is about to attend an important conference or he is waiting for the birth of his first child, you may find him too distracted. Then there are the bosses who find it convenient never to spend time with their staff. Timing with this type of boss will be tricky.

Ann Manello worked for Herb in the state education department. Every time she tried to talk to him about her concerns, he agreed that they needed to get together, but not just then. There was always an urgent meeting, a big report due. He was about to go on vacation, or had just gotten back from one. Finally, she had to wait until she and Herb were on a plane traveling to a conference in Chicago to corner him. She made sure they were seated next to each other, and as soon as the plane started to taxi for take off, she turned to him and said, "Herb, now that we have some uninterrupted time together, I am hoping we can talk about my objectives." Herb had the window seat. Ann was on the aisle. There was nowhere he could go.

Imagine yourself sending your boss an e-mail that says, "Jennifer, I need a few minutes of your time this afternoon or tomorrow morning. When can you meet with me?" If she gives you a time, good. Take the meeting. She may, however, come back to you and want to know what it's about. If your goal is to change something about the work schedule or is otherwise task oriented, tell her what you want, but in a neutral way.

Do not say: "You gave us an impossibly short deadline on the Canadian campaign."

Say: "I need your advice on how to proceed on the Canadian campaign."

In other words make it sound important *to her.*

Be Ready

Plan what you are going to say and practice ahead of time. Practice? Yes. Go over the meeting in your mind. Have a rehearsal with someone who can play the boss for you. It might be interesting to have the friend pretend she is the boss in a good mood, and then in a bad mood. One caution on this technique: It is a double-edged sword. It will allow you to go over your spiel and your questions and to envision yourself doing it in a nonthreatening atmosphere. This will set you up to succeed. But be careful not to expect that the boss will actually act the way your friend does. Too definite an expectation, especially a negative one, can color your approach and force you into a self-fulfilling prophecy. That is, that by expecting a negative reaction, you will do things, without really being conscious of them, that will elicit the disaster you expect. This is why an optimistic and confident outlook is so important to your success in this, as in anything.

Be Realistic

You need to go in with a positive expectation, but a realistic one, too. Typically, people go through three steps in responding to a problem:

- First, they say there is no problem.
- Second, they admit that there is problem, but they refuse to accept any responsibility for it.
- Third, they admit there is problem and that there is something they can do about it.

Notice that at no point in this process can we be sure that your boss will admit that the problem is his fault. Some may surprise you, but you cannot count on it, especially from someone who thinks being in charge means always being right.

Expect your boss to go through the steps above. At each step, your objective is to get her to the next step. Do not look for self-incrimination or remorse. That only happens in the movies, and as much as we can use movies as a metaphor for thinking about this problem, we have to assume that real life efforts will not necessarily end all tied up with a neat bow. Rather than tearful remorse, expect that the boss will want to come out of this meeting still feeling 100 percent in charge. Set up the situation so that a calm, businesslike discussion will satisfy both of you and allow each of you to complete the task with dignity.

Expect Surprises

Be prepared to deal with shock. Your boss may be sincerely surprised by the difficulties you recount. Remember, if the boss cannot read your mind, you cannot read hers either. She may be stunned by what you have to say. He may also react with embarrassment or nervousness. If emotionally charged situations make you flustered, understand that they do the same to your boss. Hard as it is to believe, that monster in the corner office is really a human being. If he is nervous and overreacts, don't let it steam you up. Your hopes for a peaceful solution could evaporate in the resulting heat. Be brave and patient and keep working at it.

Stay on Subject

When you choose what topics you discuss, remember that this is a work relationship. You can bring up the boss's communications with you or your need for information and feedback on your work. You can talk about work flow, the organization, your future, how someone else's behavior affects your work. Never bring up personalities—yours, the boss's, or anyone else's. You are not conducting a therapy session. Even if you have a Ph.D. in psychology and are fully qualified to psychoanalyze your boss, do not do it. If you lack a degree in psychology, you have no business analyzing anyone. Your objective in these meetings is to prevent your boss from being a menace to you, not to become a menace yourself. Keep yourself honest by talking about people—you, your boss, your coworkers, your staff—in terms of what they do and what they do not do, rather than in terms of what they are or are not. Talk about behavior, not character.

Be Diplomatic

The way you communicate matters. Be diplomatic. Follow these simple rules:

- Make sure you have positive things to say and present them in specific terms.
  Do not say: "You communicate with me very well."
  Say: "You always give me the information I need to understand the customers' needs. With the National Trust order, for instance . . ."
- When you talk about your complaints, talk about them in the future tense.
  Do not say: "You never invite me to the Friday meetings."
  Say: "I'd like to come to the Friday management meetings. I think I can learn a lot and make a contribution to the group discussion."

Clear Up Misunderstandings

Beware of misunderstandings. In many problem-solving discussions, emotions run high. Misinterpretations and miscommunications are bound to happen. If your boss says something that puzzles you, and especially if it outrages you, ask for clarity. Explain what you thought you heard, and then ask him to verify that you have understood him correctly. If your boss reacts emotionally when you think you've said something neutral, make sure she understood what you said. Not all disagreements result from misunderstandings, but the ones that do are a waste of energy. Check to make sure your communication is accurate.

Read the Signs

Watch your body language. Be sure you are not sending messages you want to conceal by crossing your arms across your chest or failing to make eye contact. And watch what your boss's gestures tell you about his attitudes. Jackie Auer had a boss who always tried to show a poker face. He had spent years as a personnel interviewer and developed a knack for hiding his feelings—he thought. Jackie did not notice it at first, but his body language gave him away. When Jackie went to see him with a new idea one day, he started to play with his tie. She did not read the cue but went on. Then her boss swiveled around in his chair and looked at her over his left shoulder. Jackie persisted. At last, he looked out the window and started playing with his tie again. When she finished what she had to say, the boss told Jackie he would consider her suggestions and get back to her. She never heard about it again.

Eventually, Jackie learned to interpret the boss's body language. When his hand went to his tie, she changed her line of attack. When he swiveled around in his chair, she asked him how he felt about what she was saying. When he looked out the window and reached for his tie, she beat a swift but graceful path to the nearest door.

Experts say you can build rapport by matching your communications style and body language to that of the person you are speaking with. Keep your voice level and tempo in sync with his. Do this if the signals you are getting are positive.

Don't do this if the signals are negative. If your boss shouts and folds his arms, you'd be foolish to copy his stance.

Approach as an Equal

If you whine like a victim, you will invite victimization. If you present yourself as an impotent sufferer, you will be dubbed as an unworthy wimp. A straightforward approach, laced with a little humor and a lot of tact, will make the most successful presentation of your point of view.

Motivate Your Boss

If you need to approach your boss for something personal, for instance to get him to stop yelling all the time, even in this situation you have to make what you say motivate him.

Do not say: "The way you behave upsets me."

Say: "I want to stay motivated and do a good job. I know that you really care about what happens around here, but for me to continue to care, I need you to talk to me in a normal tone of voice."

Be Fair

Try to strike a balance between gloom and doom and a whitewash.

- If your boss erupts like Mount St. Helens when you try to give him bad news, you may be tempted to back off. You need to tell the truth. Use the techniques of diplomacy and stick to the real story.
- But do not come across with too many problems at once. If you apply too much pressure, the boss will reject everything you say. People can become suspicious of the hard sell. If you try to rush the boss into a decision without allowing time for due consideration, she may balk and you may lose your opportunity entirely.

- Acknowledge the boss's point of view. If you are bringing up something urgent and your timing is awkward, say so: "I know this is coming at a tough time in the middle of budgeting, but I think it is important enough that you will want to discuss it now." The boss will find it easier to listen and empathize if you demonstrate that you are an understanding person yourself.

Validate Positive Behavior

Be sure to show your boss that you notice whatever good management practices she does employ. When you start out the discussion, begin with something positive if you can.

Do not say: "You never tell me what my goals should be."

Say: "I like the fact that you give me the independence to make my own decisions; it helps me learn and take more responsibility." Then you can go on to say: "There are times, however, when I feel I need more guidance."

Be Flexible

Be prepared to trade off. Know what you want, but stay flexible during this negotiation. Your boss has a viewpoint and very likely knowledge that you lack. The best solution is probably neither hers nor yours, but something that will appeal to both of you. You will never be able to discover what those mutually agreeable ideas are if you are rigid about your requests.

Be Ready to Counter Resistance

The boss may respond with any number of blocks and obstacles: "That's not the way we do it here." "This is an imposition on me." "You are not a team player." The best way to deal with objections like this is not to respond too defensively. Instead, try to get at the underlying causes of the boss's resistance and to deal with them.

However slippery your monster is, try to deal with her sincerely and honestly. Recognize and have the courage to state your feelings and observations. Say what you see and how you feel about it. Ask directly for what you want. If you and your boss are willing to work hard together, you may win out over your past difficulties.

Say: "I am being straight with you. I need you to be straight with me."

End with a Plan

End the meeting with an action plan. If the boss accepts what you say and gives you and open-minded hearing, you may be on your way to a vastly improved working relationship with your monster boss. Another useful outcome would be to set a date for your next discussion.

Follow Up

When the meeting is over, write the boss an e-mail thanking him for the opportunity and summarizing—in as positive a way as you can—your agreements.

Years ago, in the heyday of unions, many employees could go to a shop steward with grievances. Now fewer than 12 percent of American workers have that option. Most companies have a policy that says you can go to Human Resources if you have a problem. But the fact of the matter is that very few people ever take advantage of this route. People pretty much know that HR is the last stop on your way out.

Your first step needs to be trying to solve the problem yourself. The ensuing chapters give you specific ways of dealing with varieties of brutes, demons, freaks, and fiends. You are about to rehearse your role as your own hero. You need to start by rewriting your own script. And then . . .

Lights, camera, action!

4

HOW TO FIGHT BACK

"Their weapons are our weaknesses: fear, ambition, illness, pride, selfishness, desire, ignorance."

E. B. White

Rick Ianuzzi worked for Mindy, an executive vice president whose behavior so was dysfunctional and her appearance so dramatic she looked more like a cartoon villain than a corporate executive. Mindy favored pointy stiletto shoes and bright red nail polish and believed that anyone who worked for the division she ran should feel honored to be asked to take her clothes to the dry cleaners.

Besides Rick, monstrous Mindy had three other direct reports: Larry chain-smoked, overate, and had already had angioplasty at the age of forty-nine; Mary Beth drank too much at lunch; Ian popped "muscle relaxants" even when his chronic lower back pain wasn't the problem.

"Ian's pain," Rick quipped, "is Mindy, and it hits a little lower down than the small of the back." When Rick wittily skewered their boss, Mary Beth laughed too loud, and Larry and Ian shook their heads. But it wasn't all fun and games; humor was Rick's weapon of choice.

"She chooses that color on her nails so the blood won't show."
"She can bring joy just by leaving the room."
"We all know she will go far, and we cannot wait for her to start."

Humor is the human race's greatest weapon against adversity. And though his buddies more or less laughed when Rick lampooned Mindy behind her back, they didn't really get the joke. Rick did. How could he make light of a person who publicly humiliated her underlings? And she definitely thought of them as underlings.

He just shrugged and grinned wickedly. "She a witch, with a capital 'B.' Everyone knows that. I like my work. I get to design restaurants and have big budgets to do that. That's what I want to do. Mindy goes around terrorizing people. Well, I don't let it work on me. She sneers, and they crumple; she sneers at me, and I design a gorgeous bar for a steak house. They want her to admire them; I want her to sign off on my raises."

Miraculous. Rick's humor and his refusal to take Mindy's barbs to heart are his antidote for her poison.

Larry and Mary Beth swear that Mindy doesn't go after Rick as much as she does them. Now why do you suppose that is?

If Mindy feeds her evil ego by psycho-punching people, and her punches glance off Rick, she will go in pursuit of someone who groans.

Why Humor Works

What weapons does your monster boss have that work against you? Why do they work? What is it about the way you respond to the monster's poisons that makes you his victim? If he stings you and you swell up and get all red and itchy, you are truly stung. If you do not react to his venom, then—well nothing.

There are viruses that could kill a dog that are harmless for a hamster. In their various ways Larry, Mary Beth, and

Ian have let themselves become Mindy's dogs. They are allowing her bullying to slowly kill them. Mindy controls them by pushing their buttons. But with Rick, when she presses the button, nothing happens. Even the most persistent person will eventually quit and go push someone else's buttons.

Mindy has no right to have top-level people drive her to her hair appointments. The company does not pay them to take her car to be inspected. She is a loathsome brat. There may be other weapons to use against her—powerful ones that will topple her from her position of power. It would be a joy forever to see her get her comeuppance once and for all. But until that day, Rick's jokes and healthy attitude keep him from letting anger sicken or cripple him.

Humor saves lives because it takes the negative emotions out of the equation. Most of the pain your monster boss causes you has to do with things you think you need from him. You deserve respect, decent treatment. It is right that you should get them. It is not fair that you are saddled with too much work, publicly belittled, manipulated with the threat of losing your job. You are absolutely right about your rights. But being right is not going to stop your blood pressure from rising. In fact, wallowing in your negative emotions can make it go up faster. Laughing at adversity can keep it down.

Choose Your Weapon

Let's presume, at least for now, that you are going to keep this job. If you are going to improve your situation enough to make it bearable, you have to understand the war you are in—the monster's weapons and your own.

Let's start with emotional weapons. By playing on your emotions, a beastly boss controls you. By belittling your capabilities, she makes you feel hopeless, incapable of solving your own problems, afraid you could never get another job where you might find the respect you deserve. When you believe your efforts will fail, you stay where you are and suffer. Your boss uses fear to intimidate you into frozen compliance. After a while resentment sets in, but it never leads you anywhere but to more negative thinking.

Some monster bosses charm you into believing in them; they seduce you rather than bully you. You end up admiring your bosszilla and doing his bidding with no hope that she will admire you in return. She promises raises, promotions, or more challenging work. As time passes, however, her demands increase, but the raise or promotion never materializes, and you realize you've have been had. Your motivation disappears in a puff of smoke.

The awful truth is that although many of us see the boss-subordinate relationship as one involving reciprocal loyalty and admiration, for bad bosses it is a one-way street. We may take it as fundamentally human and emotionally important, but a bad boss, after years of loyal service, might cut you off without a care and even use that trite phrase: "It's not personal; it's just business." In this oft-used excuse for miserable decisions lies your answer. You have to make it "just business" to you.

Disarm the Monster

You disarm the monster by removing the most potent of his weapons—your emotions. If you never love or hate or fear him, his attacks are harmless. It is how Rick Ianuzzi stays sane in the face of Mindy's horrific behavior. He knows that some people are worth an emotional response, but she is not one of them.

This is a change within yourself that can make your work life bearable. It will not be easy to make such a change, but if you want to stay, you have to work very hard to turn off those emotional responses—you have no other choice.

Flip to the back of the book and review your objectives. Is what you want based on your emotional needs rather than your business needs? Are you really looking for admiration? Recognition? A boss who understands or cares about your problems? Love? If so, you are laying yourself open to some real potential miseries here.

The thing about Rick Ianuzzi is that he is a grown-up. Hard as it is on this planet, he has managed to pursue a career with realistic expectations. He also says this, "Poor Mary Beth. She wants Mindy to admire her. Good god. Mindy is a totally self-absorbed, small-minded person who cares about nothing but her own ambitions and the price she can pay for a handbag. I keep trying to tell Mary Beth, 'Cut it out. Who would want the admiration of a snake like her?' I only want the admiration of people I admire."

Again, brilliant. More potential armor against the barbs of an abusive boss.

What's Your Role?

Think about your own emotions and their part in this problem. You think about this situation all the time anyway, so why not make some of that thinking productive? Where did you get those unfulfilled needs that you wish the boss would take care of for you? This could be complicated for you and maybe involve experiences that went wrong for you a long, long time ago. Whatever the reason for those emotional needs, you are looking in the wrong place for an answer. You will find much more about this in the Blair Witch chapter. For now, it's enough to understand that if your expectations are that the boss will "feed your inner child," you are looking for nourishment in the wrong cupboard. In the twenty-first century workplace, you may be required to feed the boss's inner child, but it is unlikely he will be required to feed yours.

If you disarm the boss by taking away his emotional weapons, you must find your own armory for your fight for job satisfaction, career advancement, or whatever real business rewards you are looking for.

Your greatest weapon will be your own will. You can and must draw the line on abuse. Facing up to bullies makes them back down. No matter how long you have been taking an emotional shellacking and no matter how important your job is to you, it's important to stand up against insults and intimidation. In Chapter 3, we discussed how to communicate with your monster to stop the flow of invective, but knowing what to say is useless unless you actually say something. I can't state this often enough: Your number one weapon here is your will. Acting like a doormat will only encourage people to wipe their feet on you. If you approached your front door and your doormat suddenly stood up and said, "Pardon me, but you really should not be doing that to me," you would take notice.

Be Ready

Have a plan for what you will do when those familiar situations arise, when you know that your fear or ire or shame will kick in. Separate yourself from the emotions. When you see the monster walking toward you with his determined stride, the glower on his brow, the set of his chin, you may quiver with fright. Just the sight of him in attack mode may plague you with feelings of helplessness and destroy your ability to deal with him. Instead of anticipating his rage as he comes toward you, latch on to your confidence. Don't cringe. Look at your computer screen. Smile at it. Click the save button, look up, smile at him, and then say something like, "This Valley Power reco is going really well. I think it should be ready ahead of schedule."

If he becomes emotional and you remain calm, you have the advantage. If he rages and you mollify him and logically solve the problem, eventually he will back off. In any such interchange, the emotionally detached person looks and feels in charge.

If your boss rages to see you cower, and you smile instead, you will not be rewarding his behavior. Eventually, he may stop. If your calm exterior enrages him even more, if he really goes off the deep end—to the point where you feel frightened—pick up your personal belongings and leave at once. I am *not* kidding. If your boss is psychologically unbalanced, you may not be physically safe working for him.

Identify the Dysfunction

All monster bosses are dysfunctional in some way. Figure yours out. What are the specifics of his personality problem? What goes on in his mind? You do not have to psychoanalyze him. Just watch how he behaves. What sets him off? What makes him angry? What scares her? What makes her laugh? The more you know about what makes him tick, the better you will be able to manipulate or otherwise control him. Just understanding may help you cope. Knowing that he frets over his appearance, you may be able to shield yourself from his venom just by saying, "What a nice tie."

Also, learn to make yourself less of a target. Be so busy getting the work done that you are too preoccupied to look up when she comes storming into the department with her red nails sharpened for blood.

Outsmart Him

Apply the stealth methods from your childhood to the situation.

Ed Robinson claims he learned all he needed to know about manipulating his boss from watching his mother manipulate his father. "I would hear my mother talking to my grandmother on a Monday about wanting to go to visit my uncle in Philadelphia over the weekend. Then that night at dinner, she would say to my father, "We haven't seen my brother James in a long time. I wonder how they are coming with building that extension on the back of their house." Ed's father would respond with a grunt. His mom would just drop the subject. Then on Wednesday evening, she would say, "Willie, I was talking to my brother James this morning, and he says the new family room is all done, and he and Miranda would love for us to come down for a visit sometime soon." Again she wouldn't press for anything like a commitment. Thursday was her day to close the deal. "They said on the radio that the weather is going to be really nice this weekend. We ought to take advantage of it and plan to do something." Then my dad would say, "Well, why don't we take a drive down to Philadelphia to see James?"

"Oh, that would be nice," my mother would say, as if it were not her idea all the while.

Now that's what Ed Morris does with his boss. He works in an auto parts dealership and has a boss who likes to say no to everything. When he wanted to convince his boss to make an important change, he did "à la mom." He could have said, "I think we need new software for the cash registers." Instead, he started by feeding the boss stories about customers having to wait too long while the clerks process transactions. Then, at the apt moment, he slipped the boss a brochure on some new software that allows customers to swipe their own credit cards and sign electronically. Whenever there was a line in the store and the customers looked impatient, he made sure the boss heard about it. The next thing he knew, the boss was saying, "We have to do something about these lines or we are going to lose business." Voilà! The boss had a brilliant idea. "Let's install a new system that will help us process transactions faster."

I asked if Ed did not want credit for the idea, since he was the one who identified and resolved the problem. "Yeah," he said, "I guess, but on some level, I think he knows that it was my idea. Even if he doesn't, the place functions better and what the heck, I am no worse off than I was. Better really, since I do not have that long line of customers waiting out there making me nervous."

Gerry Clinton used the straw man technique on his difficult boss. "He always wanted to say no to something, so I never asked him for one thing at a time. I always asked him for three—the two I really wanted and one that would cost the most that was expendable. Typically, he approved the first two and refused the third. Worked almost every time."

Gerry and Ed both know that bosses frequently want the people who work for them to tell them what to do. They just do not, in the process, want to be made to feel stupid or that they are not totally in charge. You can get what you want from the boss, but you may have to allow her to take the credit for the great idea—or at least for recognizing the great idea.

Plan Your Escape

But before you deploy any of these weapons in the monster wars, you need to think through your escape plan. I mean write it out. You'll find a page at the back of this book for your notes. Go to it very soon and make a written plan. Focus on what you will do if you need to leave. Update your résumé. Put together a step-by-step process for how you'll find your next job and how you will exit gracefully. Make a to-do list in case you are suddenly forced to activate this plan. List Web sites where you might find a job opening, and names and contact information for everyone you can talk to about your search.

Do this diligently. When your plan is ready, it will be your fallback position. Activating it will certainly not be your first step, but just having it will make you feel more confident that you are prepared to move quickly if it comes to that. Once your plan is mapped out, you can aim your weapons at fixing the problem. If your battle plan works, that's great. If it doesn't work, you will have your next step in place.

Battle Stations

Now, to that battle plan. The more you know about what makes the monster tick, the emotions that curdle her bravado, the more weapons you will find to use against her. In scary movies, the monster is terrorizing the countryside. The camera pans back. Suddenly, the audience sees the means of the monster's destruction in the distance. That camera angle is the metaphor for your answer to a vital question. You need to step back from the situation and view your monster dispassionately. What does she want? What does he hate? Who does he fear? When you know the answers, you will see what weapons will work.

Sympathy, with an appreciation of the other person's needs and abilities, has proven the most successful technique in persuading people to see your point of view.

If they know you see their problem, they are more likely to want to listen to your perspective. They begin to see that you are on the same team after all. That realization dampens their motivation to attack you.

Knowing what your boss fears is a powerful tool. There is a reason why bad bosses often use fear to manipulate people. Fear is often an emotion they recognize. If they find you genuinely empathetic, again they will see you as on their side. But be honest and subtle. When she starts to pressure you about the report for her boss, you don't want to blurt out, "Oh, you are just as afraid of him as I am of you." You need to say, "George really liked that statistical analysis we did last month. Maybe we should give him more numbers. That will keep his hot breath off our necks."

Begin in small ways. Work your way up to the big stuff. If your boss asks you to do something that you know is stupid or counterproductive or, worse yet, something potentially harmful to you, no matter how dictatorial he is, you need to know how to avoid doing it.

Offer Alternatives

The most productive course of action, of course, is to offer alternatives. Do not be afraid. Understand that most of the harebrained schemes that bosses come up with are based on their fears. Poor little frightened bunny. Quivering in terror, his constricted brain seizes on the first thing that comes to mind. Then, the nonsense drops down onto the back of his tongue and comes spilling—unconsidered—out of his mouth.

Just because your boss said it, doesn't mean you have to do it. Being provisional, you can suggest, "What do you think of doing it this way?" Just because you fear that your little scaredy bunny will turn into a were-rabbit doesn't mean you have to obey him. The cardinal rule in business is: never whine about a problem without suggesting a solution. With monster bosses this is not only good advice, it may be your shield against being eaten alive.

Again, in a sense, your boss wants you to tell him what to do. Despite his bravado, your boss may welcome your suggestions. You have to present your ideas with confidence and respect. It should be easy to be confident since it's likely that you know more than she does about the situation.

If you cannot convince him to open up to support a better course of action, and if what he is asking is potentially harmful, you can always say "yes" but not do it, or do it "wrong," or work at it for a long, long time, without finishing it.

You can "misunderstand" what's wanted and do what you know is best. The risk here is that you will technically be insubordinate or look incompetent. Use this tactic judiciously.

Show Off

This is the Age of Human Capital. While a heinous idea in one sense—that you should be considered an asset of some company, as if it owns you—it also means that companies are finally grasping that they are composed of people—that it is the workers who give them value and create their wealth for them. Because you are valuable, you ought to be able to speak up without getting fired.

Make sure that your boss focuses on how valuable you are. You may assume he must notice how much you do and how well you do it, but you probably need to buy a little insurance in this regard. Keep her informed. Shoot her an e-mail when you finish a project. If you have ongoing work where you are fielding issues and dealing with them, give him a weekly summary on the status of your work, your major accomplishments. Keep copies of the summaries so that you can talk about them at performance appraisal time.

I am sure you realize by now that nothing we are talking about here will work unless you are a really good employee. If you are a goof-off or a major screwup, you surrender all rights in the monster wars. There are victims who do not deserve their pain, and then there are the idiotic, the arrogant, and the lazy. In a horror movie, the audience cheers when they get eaten.

5

BLOB BOSS

SPINELESS, EQUIVOCATING, COWARDLY

In the 1958 movie *The Blob*, green slime from outer space seems perfectly harmless until everyone finds out that it envelopes and eats people alive.

On her way to work one Friday, Larissa Lawler backed her car into the garage door for the second time in a month. She jumped out of the car and checked out the damage—a dent in the left rear bumper of her Passat and a crack in one of the panels of the garage door. Some telltale green paint on the door would prove whose car had done the deed. Her husband Jim would never really understand that the dent and crack were Larissa's boss's fault. The more serious dent was in Larissa's chances for a promotion; and a worse crack was beginning to form in her sanity.

That Friday of *Garage Door Crackup II* was also the date of Larissa's annual review. Apart from the ordinary performance appraisal jitters anyone would have, in reality, Larissa had nothing to worry about. She was a product manager in the marketing department of a software company and everyone knew she was great at her job. Sales were way up. All on her own, Larissa had volunteered to work with people from other departments on a team to redesign the company's Web site. Her efforts proved a big success, both with customers and with the backroom people who handled shipping and accounting. Larissa was eager to take on new challenges, but her boss, Hugh Robertson, was about as likely to push her forward as her garage door was to heal itself. Pinning Hugh down was impossible. She wasted hours thinking up rationales to get him to make an ordinary decision.

That same night, after her performance review, she complained to her husband, Jim. "Everything Hugh says is bland. He said my performance is okay. He gave me a wishy-washy raise. When I told him what my career objectives were, he gave me that same benign smile I see every time I suggest innovation. He offers no direction, no enthusiasm, and no support." She picked up a paring knife and chopped carrots with a vengeance. "The dynamic world of technology," she moaned. "We should be go-go-go in my department. Instead, we spend hours talking around in circles. Hugh is our age, for heaven's sake. But he moves like he is a hundred."

"But he seems so nice," Jim said, Larissa was sure for the hundredth time.

Unfortunately, this summed up Larissa's problem. Hugh never yelled or screamed; most of the time he seemed so kind. In the beginning, Larissa thought he was great. He never disagreed with her. Then she saw that he never disagreed with anyone about anything—no matter how mutton-headed they, or their ideas, were. Though he always seemed to agree with her, he never carried through on his promises. Yes, he thought the package copy on the accounting software should be redesigned, but he never brought it up with the design department and never got anyone to do anything about it. It was like working in a weightless atmosphere. Anything that arrived on Hugh's desk seemed to just float away into outer space.

Hugh was a huge gooey obstacle between Larissa and progress. And she might as well beat her head against the garage door as try to get him to stand up for anything.

Identifying Blob Behavior

Larissa has a boss who has melted into a gelatinous nothingness. The man is a blob. This kind of boss appears harmless, fair-minded, and pleasant—that's how he draws you in—but he is harboring some very negative traits. Initially, he appears benign; if he has sharp claws, you don't see them. You leave a job interview feeling certain this person will be the boss of your dreams. You can tell that he won't yell or scream. Blobs do not insult their employees or crush their hopes with nasty rejections. Like the gummy green creature in the movie made in the 1950s, these bosses don't make a lot of noise. They are silent, but deadly.

Their easy-going management style may be hiding massive insecurity, limited intelligence, or an inability to make decisions and take action. They may remain pleasant and genuinely kind, but they prove indecisive and unable to commit—leaving you trapped beneath their mind-numbing ineffectiveness. A blob boss becomes a gelatinous roadblock to your bright future. They never communicate clearly, except by their actions—and their actions say "Not now, I'm resting." Are they stupid? Are they lazy? Are they so scared of their bosses that they are frozen into petrified inaction? Or is it all of the above?

Some bosses without backbones are simply not that bright. They make decisions without understanding consequences and will not budge from their wrong-headedness. Although they may seem unable to understand concepts immediately apparent to a six-year-old owner of a lemonade stand, being wrong does not intimidate them. They don't know they are wrong. They don't know that they don't know. There is practically no problem so simple that it can't confuse them.

These bosses often become mired in trivia, making mountains of work out of molehills of minutia and, in the process, molehills of profit out of mountains of investment. They become detail drones who overdramatize insignificant issues, frustrate their staff, and waste everyone's time. These bosses squash motivation by paying slavish attention to minor rules and overcomplicating simple procedures. Unable to analyze and evaluate, blobby bosses frequently cannot recognize a good idea when they hear one. They prefer to make decisions based on precedent, and they distrust anything new. Most people fear the unknown, but blobby bosses know almost nothing, so they fear almost everything. They greet every creative thought with suspicion and misgiving. They keep the word "no" on a hair trigger.

Typically, these bosses never offer ideas. They agree with everything, but deliver on nothing. They offer no leadership, and they've got no moxie. They rarely leave you feeling afraid for your safety, but they make work frustrating and boring.

Corporate Reality

There is a caveat here. If you need a lot of structure and definition and your boss's approach to the business is fluid, your needs may be in conflict with current business trends. If what you want from your boss is less flexibility, you may not be the victim of the Blob; your expectations may be more in alignment with an "old-fashioned" corporate structure. Twenty years ago, well-managed firms typically had formal, hierarchical organization charts; closely defined job descriptions; and salary charts with minimums, midpoints, and maximums. Recently, especially in the most competitive, creative, and innovative organizations, those rules are considered counterproductive, staid, and rigid. Some modern corporations have abandoned these conventions of orderliness for a more freewheeling approach. If you work for one of these organizations, and you want your boss to clearly define the parameters of your responsibilities (so you know exactly what is expected of you), you may be on a collision course with today's corporate culture.

If you worked at IBM in the 1980s, for example, you probably got used to a carefully structured workplace—no guesswork about who was responsible for what or who made the decisions about what. It was all very predictable. But now IBM and other companies like it are competing on a global scale. They feel they have to be lighter on their feet. They are jettisoning corporate structures of the past and replacing them with more open organizations where employees, once they understand the goals, are encouraged to take responsibility for their own work. Self-management is one result. Another is groups formed around a team project, where the members of the group organize themselves to get the job done. In these companies, bosses typically don't stringently define each employee's duties. Your boss's definition of what the job is may seem bland or amorphous, but that is part of the paradigm of these modern corporations.

On the other hand, it may be your boss who is suffering from future shock. If you arrived on the job already attuned to this twenty-first-century concept, and you acquired a blobby boss, it may be a result of his being in a state of shock over how the typical American corporation has changed. A person totally invested in outdated expectations could feel completely disoriented, particularly if his corporate structures and processes are in an unprecedented state of flux. This may be the reason your boss remains ineffective and incapable of making decisions or taking action. If his old reliable expectations and rules were dissolved in the last decade or so, maybe he dissolved right along with them.

Where They Reside

You don't typically find blobs operating as heads of corporations or even small businesses, primarily because it is hard to sustain a business if its head has melted into a gluey mess. You will, however, find many in corporate middle management. How does this happen? Your typical blob is, after all, bland. Unfortunately, it works this way: Mangers who want nonthreatening subordinates in first-line supervisory positions choose nonthreatening employees to oversee small parts of the organization. Or perhaps, there were three candidates for a supervisory job. Two of them were strong, and each was favored by some of the people in a position to decide, but because the decision was in conflict, they compromised on the least threatening person—the blob.

Sometimes blobs are promoted based on seniority, simply because they hang around so long. The Peter Principle is often responsible. This theory, popularized in the 1980s by the book of the same name, says that in hierarchical organizations managers continue to receive promotions until they reach their level of incompetence. The Peter Principle is alive and well and seems to explain why a lot of nincompoops end up in jobs they never deserved.

Strategies for Coping with an Ineffective Boss

Even if your boss has melted into that annoying gelatinous state of nothingness and you are living in a constant state of frustration, all is not lost. If you steer clear enough to avoid being swept under, you can avoid becoming a victim. You need to identify the problems, assess where they are coming from, and strategize so that you can keep your ambitions intact and make progress in your career. If you're smart and deliberate, you can prevent the blob from smothering your best qualities.

Go Around Him

If your boss is behaving like a blob by blocking every bold idea you have, consider going around him. Since this can be risky, first be sure that you have thought your scheme through. Make sure you know the downside risks of what you are proposing and that you are prepared to face them. Then, as long as what you want to do is benign, productive, and not outside the budget, go ahead and do it the way you know it needs to be done. For instance, if your boss tap dances every time you ask for permission to change anything, and you know that reorganizing the shipping room will help everyone work more efficiently, instead of asking his permission, reorganize it, and let him see the efficiencies gained from doing it your way.

Be Proactive

Suppose you go to your boss with a problem, and she shakes her head and says, "That's terrible, but there's nothing we can do about it." With this boss, you need to stay on the move. Take the initiative and get out from under her repressive passivity.

If your ineffectual boss cannot be clear about anything, make up your own mind and take action. Solve problems yourself, use your creativity, and develop your own skills. Eventually one of two things will happen. Higher-ups will notice that you are the dynamo, and you will get to move ahead and away from her for good. Or you will get so good at what you do, that you can take your skills to an organization that will appreciate them.

If your lazy boss sits around whining all day long, find ways to be productive, to contribute to the company's goals beyond the doldrums. And make sure what you are doing gets noticed by people outside of your boss's group. Larissa had the right idea when she nominated herself for the Web site redesign team. Try this tactic yourself. Join groups where you can work with people from other departments.

Let Your Light Shine

If you are smarter than your boss, then use your superior intelligence for more than coming up with clever ways to describe your blob boss to your friends. Figure out the opportunities that are going unexploited because your boss is such a lump of inactivity. Get into the game by figuring out how to take advantage of the possibilities that are out there for the company and for yourself. Start projects on your own. Just be careful of high-risk issues. If what you are contemplating is going to commit the company to something risky, you do not want to put yourself at risk, too. Get permission. If the blob refuses to do anything but block your way, find a sympathetic person to talk to—a colleague with more experience, a peer in another department that will be affected by the idea you are touting. Get opinions from others before you move forward into territory where you cannot foresee the consequences of taking a certain action.

For instance, if you think an FTP site will help you and your colleagues communicate more efficiently with your clients, your first step would be to run the idea past your boss. But if your particular blob is a techno- as well as other kinds of an idiot, she may squelch your idea without even trying to understand it. One response to this rejection would be to go and have a beer with your brother-in-law and complain that you are smarter than she is and that you should be the boss. How productive would that be?

Suppose instead that you went on your own, informally, to someone in the IT department and told her about your idea, explained how you think it would work, and asked if she thought it had merit. Then, perhaps, the two of you could work out a way for the suggestion to move forward. Maybe the IT people could bring it through channels to your boss. Or maybe the head of IT needs to push for it so the boss doesn't stop it before its merits are truly evaluated. If you are determined, you can find a method for implementing your good ideas without being insubordinate or exceeding your authority.

Beware of Hidden Dangers

Warning: the goop may try to piggyback on your progress. He may suddenly wake up from his stupor when he sees you getting ahead by actually accomplishing extraordinary work and putting ideas into practice. He may very well try to take the credit! Do not panic. People around you are bound to notice that nothing came out of his lair until you pushed open the door. Keep your light shining, even if some of it reflects onto the blob and makes her look brighter than she is. Eventually, the higher-ups will figure out that you are the source of the light and that she is just a dull orb circling your bright ideas.

Offer Solutions

If your blob dwells on problems, not solutions, don't make matters worse by bringing her problems without having solutions at hand. Present her with a full package: the issue (do not call it a problem at all; most blob-bosses get even blobbier when they hear that word), the alternatives, the pros and cons, and your recommendation. This is not to say that presented with all this logic and brilliant analysis, your mucilaginous manager will actually make a decision. You may have to do that for him.

Do that for him? Yes. And that is one of the good things about working for a globule. Rigid micromanagers will never let you make a decision on your own. But the spongy among us are pliable. You can be the one who leads them.

MATT'S STORY

Matt Lipari worked for a person he described as a human jack-o'-lantern. He smiled at everything. "He is fit to be a greeter at Wal-Mart," Matt says of him, "not the head of a department in a high school." But that's what Walter is, and worse yet, he has to represent the teachers who work under him at district curriculum meetings.

That means the pleasant but ineffectual Walt is charged with representing topics that the teachers in Matt's department care about passionately. Passion is exactly what we want teachers to feel. We want what they teach to be extremely important to them. Their level of commitment and caring is critical to the quality of the education in Matt's school. But Walter, who should be leading and reinforcing their zeal, has, as Matt describes him, "No spine. Maybe he doesn't even have any bones. When the biology teachers talk about an 'askeletal creature,' they are talking not about worms but about Walt."

Matt says that his fellow teachers thought Matt was stupid for trying to change Walt. Maybe. But Matt tried anyway. He engaged Walt in conversations about the difficulties of meeting with the curriculum committee. Matt discovered that Walt was scared to death of taking a stand because he didn't want to alienate anyone. Walt felt safe only if no one disagreed with him. He coped by never taking a strong position on anything. Matt came up with an idea on how to solve the problem. He wrote a position paper, documenting the opinions of the teachers, for Walt to take to the curriculum meetings. That way Walt was able to express their ideas not in terms of his own opinions, but as the consensus of his group.

From time to time, Walt even asked Matt to represent him at the meetings. "When I attend the meetings," Matt says, "I can push harder for what the teachers in our school really want. I don't think Walt will ever fight as hard as we want him to, but this way at least our thoughts get to weigh in some. That's better than what was going on before."

Eventually, Matt volunteered to work with a committee over the summer to hammer out some of the differences. In a way he was doing part of Walt's job, which wasn't quite fair, but it got the job done better than Walt would have done it.

This is not the best possible outcome, but it is progress. If you have a spongy supervisor, you may be able to get him to absorb some of what you say, and at least regurgitate it for the powers that be. Give it a try.

Pin Her Down

If your mushy manager is never clear on what she says, take the initiative to clear up her pudding-headed communications. For example, if you have just met to establish new goals, she might be typically evasive and noncommittal by saying, "We ought to be able to get this done in a reasonable amount of time."

Rather than agree to a nebulous goal, you can quickly counter with, "Do you think we can complete this by the end of the month?" Being gelatinous, she will probably reply by saying something innocuous like, "I guess so."

This is where you nail it down by saying, "Okay, July thirty-first will be the due date." Then, dash to your desk and shoot her an e-mail to confirm the goals and the date.

When to Surrender

It's one thing trying to work around a boss who is lazy or has no backbone or leadership abilities, but it's quite another problem if what you have to contend with is a critter with no bones *and* no brains. If your gloppy boss is just plain dumb, you can try reversing roles with him, but that will work only if he is a true blob—dumb and pliable. If he is dumb and digs his heels in and will not let you use your intelligence to get anything done, well, run for your life. Why waste your time working for such a cipher?

This is 100 percent true if this person runs the company. How, you ask, could such an ineffectual person get a job running a company? My best guess would be that he inherited it. Since some degree of merit and dynamism is required to get a shot at the top spots, blobs seldom rise to the highest-level positions in large organizations in any other way. In situations where they do take charge, the whole organization is likely to become one big blob. As I said, run away.

One of the most stressful things a blob-boss can do is to shy away from correcting people. If you are doing your job and working hard, nothing is quite as frustrating as watching your coworkers get away with murder. You wind up dealing with all the irate customers while the other people in your work group surf the net for bargains in beachwear. This is about the thorniest problem a blob boss can face you with. What can you do: rat on your fellow employees and try to get him to scold them? Scold them yourself? I would think neither of those would be comfortable or productive. You can try one thing and one thing only: try to engage them in serious work, not by bossing them or correcting them, but by asking them questions and seeing if they can "help" you get some of the work done. What a dreadful position to have to be in. But it may be your only hope. Your other options are to put your head down and do your job. Or to quit. You may think quitting is a drastic option, but here is the danger: watching everyone else goof off and get away with it will turn you into a blob. That green goop in the movie gets bigger every time it absorbs someone!

Remember what the cop said to Steve McQueen: "Stay away from it. As far as you can."

6

FRANKENSTEIN

TOO MANY BOSSES, TOO LITTLE TIME

"I created it. I made it with my own hands from the bodies I took from graves, gallows, anywhere."

Dr. Henry Frankenstein in *Frankenstein*

The point here is that Frankenstein's monster is not one person. He is made from many, cobbled together in a mad attempt to create a human being out of miscellaneous parts gathered from scary sources. Sometimes, maybe often, working for a number of different bosses at the same time can feel like working for a monster made up of organs taken from mental defectives and convicted criminals, not to say the dead and buried.

The days when a person had one boss, only one person who had the authority to assign work, appraise performance, and decide on raises or promotions, are a thing of the past in many corporations. For at least a decade now corporate structure has been increasingly built around work teams—organized around projects, pieces of business, client relationships. This modern team approach has a lot of advantages—it makes the group lighter on its feet, able to respond as a team to opportunities and problems, and it gives the company a number of efficiencies in staffing. The disadvantage is that the person who has several bosses assigning him work can be stymied by an overload of work and conflicting priorities.

Luz Lopez had a hard time. In her first job out of college, she went to work in a small ad agency where the staff was assigned to teams, each of which worked for different clients. Luz was assigned to work with account executives (AEs): Al on a cell phone account; Simone on advertising for an online wine seller; and Ajami on an insurance client account. About 60 percent of the time, working for three different people on three different pieces of business did not faze Luz in the least. The work for each of the clients ebbed and flowed; when one account was busy the others were less so. Plus, Luz was usually extremely well organized. She got encouraging feedback from all three of her AEs. She liked the stimulation and opportunities to learn from a variety of assignments and managers. She felt good—most of the time. But then crunch time would come, and a ton of work would land on her desk from all three—enough from each one to keep her really busy for days on end—and each AE expected a quick turnaround. Luz felt overwhelmed.

When it got to be too much for her, Luz didn't know what to do. She didn't want to make waves. She liked her job—the work and the people—and she wanted to succeed. Everyone else in the department seemed to manage their workloads and just keep going, but she felt swamped. The HR person who hired her had told her that the agency structure might mean that she would get too much work from time to time. She had said it was Luz's responsibility to make sure that her three AEs coordinated her assignments. Luz wanted to solve the problem, but she did not see any of the other account assistants complaining. She did not want to be the only one.

She limped along, never saying anything to anyone until Simone chided her for not being on time with a click-through analysis. This report indicated how many potential customers actually logged on to a client's Web site after receiving a promotional e-mail. It was the critical measure of all the agency's efforts for Simone's client. Luz knew it was very bad form for them to be late delivering the report. "I have a lot going on right now," was all Luz was able to blurt out as an explanation.

Simone reminded Luz that it was her responsibility to coordinate her work and stormed off, mumbling something about how angry the client would be if the report wasn't done on time. Luz felt alternately ashamed and angry. She felt put upon, as if all her "superiors" were being unreasonable by asking her to be the one to keep everything straight. After all, she was the newest person in the department. After this sort of thing happened a couple of times, she thought about quitting.

Identifying Frankenstein Behavior

If you have more than one boss and your multiple bosses don't communicate with you—or each other—you are in a Frankenstein situation. You will sometimes, maybe always, be overwhelmed because each of the people you report to thinks of you as his and his alone. If they don't confer with each other and coordinate with you, their expectations will be totally unreasonable and you will be left swept away in a tsunami of conflicting demands and complaints.

Corporate Reality

A loose team structure may be confusing, but it is also liberating. Often, upper management imposes this organizing principle on work groups precisely to liberate them. They want people to take initiative, to use their creativity to get things done effectively, to invent new ways to accomplish the organization's goals.

Upper management's objective may be to make people more collegial and equal and give them more flexibility. If that is not working in your case, it may be because the company seeks to do this by executive fiat—they expect that, *zap*, the CEO makes an announcement and, *bing*, everyone immediately adopts the new approach and adapts to it. Too bad the real world doesn't work that way. Top executives need to do more than make pronouncements; they need to manage for this sort of change and provide leadership that will allow new teams to learn to function well. If they do not, middle managers may not get the idea. Your bosses may be trying to function as if they were still in a hierarchical structure where someone has supremacy. Without the proper management of the change in expectations, your team members may compete instead of cooperating. Under these circumstances, teams cannot fuse. Instead of fusion, you get confusion, people being resentful, working at cross-purposes.

Strategies for Coping with Frankenstein

Part of Luz's problem in dealing with her Frankenstein was that she was new and eager to please. Dealing with multiple bosses takes confidence. You have to have the guts to speak up for yourself or you will set yourself up to fail by taking on an impossible load and never rectifying your bosses' unrealistic expectations. Here is what to do.

Communicate Workloads

If you have multiple bosses, the first tactic is to communicate your workload to each of them. Let's go back to Luz's story to illustrate this point. Things finally came to a head during one grim period. She was looking decidedly down in the mouth when the HR manager happened to see her. She asked Luz to meet with her.

"What's up?" she asked

Luz said she really liked the company, her work, her coworkers, and the clients.

"Really?"

Hesitant to complain, Luz tried to smile, but the HR manager waited so long Luz finally fessed up. "I know you said it's up to me to manage them, but I do not know where to start. I have asked them to meet with me as a group, so they can work out their priorities, but they never all seem to be available at the same time."

The HR manager suggested a way around this that was so simple that Luz was embarrassed that she hadn't thought of it herself.

Clarify Expectations

The next time Luz faced a deluge of work, she sent the following e-mail to all of them:

"Hi everyone. Today is one of those crunch days, and I am afraid there is no way I can get everyone's assignments done. Al, you asked me to gather all the recall studies, analyze the results, and write up a comparison of the fifteen-second and thirty-second spots. That in itself could take all day. And Simone, you asked me to research competitive Web sites and look at the graphics of our proposal to make sure ours is distinctive. Considering all the Web-based companies that sell wine, that is a big undertaking, too. And Ajami, we have the e-mail push that is supposed to happen next week. I am supposed to be coordinating with tech support to get everything ready.

"I need you all to tell me which of these should get the highest priority and who might be able to help me with some of it. I do not want to mess up any of it, but I cannot do it all, not today."

The most important sentence was her last, "Please click 'respond to all' with your answer so we can all stay in the loop on this."

Encourage Boss-to-Boss Communication

In Luz's case, it took a few passes, but eventually the account executives figured out a schedule that worked. Going forward, these e-mail conferences became the norm. Luz learned enough to get all three of them to be proactive, giving her assignments ahead of schedule so whenever possible they avoided last-minute crunches. By the time of her six-month review, she had the situation under control. "I used to feel whipped, but now I've whipped them into shape," she told HR.

Anticipate Problems

Once Luz felt confident in her right to speak up, she took control. She saw she was the only person who knew enough about what was going on to blow the whistle when an emergency was coming. "I used to think they should know," she reflected. "They were more experienced, in managerial positions. Now I see that they had no idea, and no motivation to find out. I was the one with the problem. I had to be the one with the solution."

Be a Smooth Politician

In a way Luz was lucky. Al, Simone, and Ajami pitched in and helped to figure out whose work should take priority. If your bosses will not confer or you despair that they will ever agree, you may need a trickier response. If the direct approach doesn't work after a couple of attempts, do what you did when you were a teenager. You remember how when you wanted to go somewhere, you got Mom to think that Dad had said yes, and Dad to think that Mom had said yes. Playing one person off against another may seem underhanded. Still, you may have to stoop to such tactics to manage bosses who are essentially working at cross-purposes. Your goal here has to be high-minded—not just to get what you want in a selfish way. If all you want is more time to play solitaire on your office computer, forget it. But if you want to get your job done properly, help the organization meet its goals, improve the quality of the work and the success of the team, or protect your health and sanity, go for it. Use the route of the midnight requisition to get the job done and preserve your own health and sanity.

Try this: Tell them all—one by one—that you need permission to arrange your own priorities. When the first one starts to look pained and cannot come up with an answer, suggest that maybe you should ask one of the others. When you have talked to all of them, do what you know is best and let them all think that everyone else said yes. A huge part of succeeding with this loose structure is knowing who among the people you work with has the most clout.

RUTHIE'S STORY

Ruthie Johnson picked the wrong favorite. She worked for a real Frankenstein crowd. Her team of product researchers in a food company seemed to have been put together by a mad scientist. Henry's energy level was so sluggish one could almost imagine that he had emerged from a grave. Elizabeth came across as so cold she might have been locked in a freezer for years. They competed with one another and used Ruthie as a way of gaining supremacy in the pecking order—especially Elizabeth, who seemed to think she was better than everyone because she had a name-brand Ph.D.

But her third boss, Victor, was generous and cooperative. He taught Ruthie things. Not like the other two who seemed to care nothing about her. Victor told her she was good at her job: the others never did anything but complain. So Ruthie responded to all three of them in kind. She let Henry keep to himself. If he asked for anything, she did not put much energy into it. With Elizabeth, she maintained a chilly distance. But she took special pains with Victor's work. Without thinking much about it, she gave Victor's projects the bulk of her attention.

If you asked Victor, he would have said that Ruthie was a near-perfect employee. The problem is that no one ever asked Victor. Elizabeth alone reviewed her performance, and Elizabeth saw her as mediocre. A lackluster report went into Ruthie's personnel file, and she got only a so-so raise.

Know the Score

By rights, everyone on a team should review an employee's performance. But even if that had happened in Ruthie's situation she would have scored low with two out of the three.

It would be only natural for you to be nicest to those who are nicest to you. On a personal level, this makes sense. But in business, that could hit you in the pocketbook. If you are not sure who among your teammates will review your performance, it is fair to ask. Find out who keeps the scorecard and make an informed decision. Better yet, do not play favorites under any circumstances. Instead, find out what tasks mean the most to the goals of the organization and give them true priority. If the company thrives, so should your personal bottom line.

When to Surrender

The difficulties of flexible team structure are bad enough for people with an independent nature and a lot of self-confidence. If you need high levels of security and predictability to feel safe, a flexible team structure could make you disoriented or freeze you with fear of failure.

What will help reorient you are clear goals, an understanding of where the organization is headed and how you are expected to help it get there. If your management does not readily give you this information, ask for it. When you get it, everything should fall into place and conflicting issues should no longer overstress you.

If you ask for clearly defined objectives and no one will give them to you, you are on the deck of a ship and no one is at the helm. In that case, take the advice of Dr. Frankenstein's father, who said, "You will soon feel better, when you get out of here."

7

BIGFOOT

CRITICAL, PUTS YOU DOWN

Bigfoot is a huge mythological apelike creature who reputedly walks uprIght, looks somewhat human, and leaves giant footprints. He is known to Native Americans as Sasquatch, which means Boss of the Mountains.

Zack Niebaum earns his living painting scenery for a TV production company that films a blockbuster television series. He belongs to a union, but jobs like his are hard to come by, and his boss, Hal, takes full advantage of his crewmembers' rampant job insecurity.

Despite the vagaries of the industry, Zack loves his work. He gets to use his artistry to create the mood for world-famous shows. If the script calls for an apartment to look grungy, Zack can make a brand new wall look as if its paint job is twenty years old. After years on his cop drama, he can create "blood spatters" that would fool a real medical examiner. Sometimes, he imagines he is spattering Hal's blood.

As scenic chargeman, Hal does everything he can to further his own career by wringing the talents and effort of his crew. He does the job as cheaply as possible with the fewest number of people, forcing everyone to put in hard days and long nights. People who toil behind the scenes expect that. But Hal makes an art form of squelching his crew. He is completely inflexible about hours. TV crews typically work twelve- or thirteen-hour days, but if a crewmember takes a day off for an emergency, Hal threatens to fire him. His credo is "Show up, or ship out." Every once in a while he fires someone—perhaps just to be mean, perhaps to set an example. The union requires Hal to offer his crew regular breaks, but Hal times those breaks to the minute.

Guys like Zack try to take that sort of thing in stride. Working in New York City, Zack has spray-painted the side of a viaduct at 2:30 A.M. in a bad neighborhood, and he has gone to work at 4:30 A.M. to make a plywood mantelpiece look as if it's made of mahogany and marble. He is proud of his ability to do that. Who wouldn't be?

"But Hal stomps all over our creativity. That's what really gets me," he says.

"One of Hal's favorite lines is, 'Why do I have to have all the good ideas?'" Hal sets out purposely to destroy his crew's confidence—not just by playing into their normal job-loss anxiety, but by also questioning their artistic competence.

Zack describes his worst time with Hal as pure psychological abuse. Hal always micromanaged their projects, which robbed his people of any creativity in what they did. "It was obvious Hal did not have any confidence in me," Zack said, "so I was losing belief in myself. Creativity requires a certain amount of trust and gut instinct. How could I be creative waiting for a big foot to crush me?"

Then Hal's Bigfoot behavior took a creative turn of its own. Zack's self-assurance was at its lowest ebb when all of sudden, instead of telling him every little thing he was to do, Hal started to be extremely vague about what was required. He withheld script information that would help Zack get things right.

This torture reached a head when they were on location at a farm upstate. The property included a barn that was in quite good condition. Hal pointed to it and said, "Zack, make that look fifty years old." Zack opened his mouth to ask a question, but before he could get out a word, Hal was walking away and grumbling, "And don't say you need me to tell you exactly how to do that."

Zack fumed. What was the scene at this place supposed to represent in the story? That was important. He could make the barn look old and charming or old and dilapidated, as if it belonged to poor framers, or he could make it look old and scary. Were the detectives going to find a body buried in it? Or did it belong to the victim's prosperous and loving parents? Hal wasn't going to tell him anything without publicly humiliating him, and rather than insist and be belittled, Zack spent the morning doing his best. "I might as well have been painting in the dark," he said.

That afternoon, when the camera guys and the art director were setting up for the shot at the barn, Hal stepped in and sneered. "How stupid is this? The whole mood and tone are off." He grabbed a can of charcoal gray paint and touched up Max's work, making himself look like a set decorating genius and making Zack look and feel like an idiot.

Identifying Bigfoot Behavior

There are *bazillions* of bosses like Hal. They give orders, not direction. They discredit their staff to build up their own reputations. They never let their people take the initiative, or they give them so little information to go on that they set them up to fail. They deny everyone else's contribution. Why would a boss want an employee to fail? To have a reason to get rid of him? To make himself look like the only competent person around? Either way, these destructive Bigfoots endanger their employees and often the project they all work on.

Instead of inspiring employees to be great, they force them to be small. They have to know better than everyone else on every topic. They see their employees' self-confidence, not as an asset to employ, but as a threat they must eliminate through intimidation and one-upmanship, by giving their people all the dumb jobs and keeping anything that requires intelligence and gains showy attention for themselves. The phrase "My way or the highway" was invented just for them.

The quintessential Bigfoot boss has a huge ego, often combined with apelike morals. These putdown artists leave giant footprints all over the self-esteem of their underlings, and make no mistake about it, *underlings* is how this variety of monster boss views his employees. Native American myth called Bigfoot "Boss of the Mountains." All Bigfoot bosses think of themselves as king of the hill. They are the put-down experts who feed their own egos by assassinating other people's sense of self. It is estimated that 20 percent of bosses bully their employees. More people complain about this type of boss than any other.

All bosses have to critique their employees. This criticism is supposed to help a person improve. Tactless Sasquatch supervisors use critiques as a way to hurt, humiliate, and belittle their employees. They criticize in front of others, are sarcastic and insulting, more hostile than helpful.

Some Bigfoot bosses are so defensive they take any suggestion as a challenge. If in fact someone shows them to be wrong, they can become even harsher. They may make their employees take the blame for their mistakes.

Often these bosses have no idea of the role they play in the "failure" of their employees. They hire the wrong person for a job and take no responsibility when he doesn't work out. They will put square pegs in round holes and then beat them on the head to make them fit.

Corporate Reality

The United States still has some old-fashioned companies, like UPS, where most of the top management started out at the bottom of the organization. Those executives under-stand what it means to be a driver for the company. They know full well how the person in brown who shows up at cus-tomers' doors is the company's best ambassador. They even brag about that in the company's advertising.

Unfortunately, though, more and more companies are managed by people who have no relationship at all with the staff at lower levels. They typically come from other compa-nies to take over managerial jobs. They move in different social spheres than the day-to-day employees. This creates a breeding ground for bosses who, by virtue of the fact that they make more money, see themselves as somehow funda-mentally better than the people they manage. Managers, especially CEOs, live in swankier neighborhoods, send their kids to exclusive private schools, and, because they live and move in these privileged places, do not identify at all with the lives of their employees. Their educations may also encour-age this social distance. MBA programs focus their students on the stockholders—not on employees or even on custom-ers. A boss with a superiority complex can easily become a bully, a Darwinian who is certain he alone is the fittest. If your boss sees you as an inferior, he may think he somehow has the right to humiliate you with demeaning work. And so the bully boss is born.

One of the greatest risks for organizations is that bosses who are bullies will never get bad news that may save them from making bad decisions. They make everyone so afraid of them that no one will ever warn them if they are headed for a cliff. In historically "successful organizations" where dominance is the management style, like the mafia or medi-eval kingdoms, there has always been recognition of this danger. Mob bosses have consiglieri, kings and dukes who ruled absolutely in the Middle Ages had court jesters to get the bad news through. If your boss will not listen to anyone with an idea different from his own, the whole organization will suffer from his mistaken decisions based on inadequate information.

The awful part about this is that your boss is supposed to be the opposite of all of this. She should be supportive. She should be helping you to succeed, keeping your motivation flowing, making you feel good about what you accomplish at work. Instead, this boss's browbeating and disparagement create cramped productivity, depression, and resentment.

One of the most important aspects of a well-run organization is the sense of community among the people who work there. The cohesiveness of your work group makes life on the job so much more rewarding than it otherwise would be. Working cooperatively with people one likes and respects toward a shared goal is one of the greatest pleasures on this planet. Even watching others do this—as in team sports—completely engages people. Work should provide this for us. Good managers foster their employees' sense of meaning and community at work. But the worst kind of Bigfoot bosses not only fail to create this atmosphere, they actively destroy it. They destroy friendships and mutual support among employees.

Strategies for Coping with a Bigfoot

If your boss divides, rather than unites, and stirs up feuds among employees, there are a couple of things you can try to stop the toxic atmosphere. If you have any hope that he will understand what you mean, tell him that he needs to unite the people in your group, that you will all work together and do better work if you can form bonds of mutual support and respect. Do not accuse him of anything. Just talk about what is positive that can be done in the future. It's worth a shot. If he refuses or gets angry with you for suggesting this, you will know how intransigent and defensive he is.

If you fail to modify her behavior, you can refuse to play her game. You can stop the divisiveness. Go to your fellow employees and describe what you think is happening and say you do not want to be part of it. Do not accuse the boss directly. Talk about the situation in general terms—state that people are working at cross-purposes, developing conflicts with one another. Start with the easiest person to approach and begin to heal the rifts. Do not leave anyone out. This effort has to include the whole team, even people you have thought you disliked. You do not have to admire them, but you do have to include them. I have seen magic happen when people make up their minds to coalesce. I am not saying it doesn't take effort, but I have seen people who thought they had a "personality conflict" come to respect and even like one another. This should be your goal.

You are thinking: why me? Why should you be the one to make this happen? You are not the boss, so it is not really your job. On the other hand, if you learn to do this and you actually accomplish it, you will have learned a skill that will help you feel confident and make you valuable to any group you ever work with. They will know you as a person who brings people together, who takes the initiative to solve problems. In other words, you will be known as a person with potential.

JOEL'S STORY

Joel Steinberg had a boss who did it all. Joel said, "He couldn't manage his own mouth, much less the company." Joel's Bigfoot was hostile to everyone. He humiliated people for sadistic satisfaction. He said no to everything, and if anyone had the audacity to ask for a reason, he said he was being objective. He used profanity and was as inflexible as ice. The average employee lasted four months. Joel figured anyone who stayed longer was either just as crazy as Herman, or had some problem that made it impossible for them get other jobs. "Sometimes I wondered if the people who stuck around were ex-cons or something. If they could have gotten another job, I imagine they would have. Whatever their defects, they couldn't be worse then my grandfather."

Yes, that's right. Poor Joel. His nasty boss was his own grandfather. And his blood relationship did not save him from being victimized along with everyone else. But his fellow employees seemed to consider him somehow responsible for his grandfather's bizarre anger. Even though he was not a manager and had no possibility of getting Herman to agree to anything, the other people in the company would ask Joel to put in all their requests and to redress their grievances.

For the first few months after he joined the company, right out of college, Joel actually tried to help. This only made Herman pick on Joel even more than he did everyone else. Joel went through a lot of changes during that time. He would hate his grandfather with all his heart. He would work himself up to a lather with his friends, telling them what he was going to do to make his grandfather just as miserable as he felt. He suffered headaches and insomnia. He thought about quitting. He thought about stealing money from the company and running away to Fiji. Eventually, he found a way to survive and stay in the company. He concentrated on learning the business well enough to take over when his grandfather could no longer dominate it.

Become a Student

Though it took Joel a long time to figure out how to endure, his method was really quite simple. He put down his head and did his job. He inured himself to his grandfather's ranting. Whenever Herman went into one of his tirades, Joel concentrated on the task at hand. He read books on how to be a good manager, and when Herman said something awful, he imagined how he would handle the same situation more productively. In this way, Joel wound up learning from the experience instead of becoming its victim. Life working for Herman wasn't fun, but it did not make Joel crazy or turn him into a thief and an absconder. He studied what worked and did not work in family businesses large and small: from Ford, Benetton, and the *New York Times* to small mail-order companies and local restaurants. When his time came to take over the family business, he was prepared to give it real leadership.

Even if your bully is not going to leave you the business in his will, you can do the same. Between now and when you can get out from under his big foot, concentrate on learning everything you can so you can take valuable knowledge—of the business, of management techniques, of yourself—with you when you get your next job.

Be in Charge of You

Some bullies got that way on the playground in the first grade. If this is the case with your boss, I am afraid he is a bully for life. But remember that the best way to treat bullies is not to be cowed by their intimidations. If you do not quiver when your bully boss starts in on you, she is likely to give up and go bully someone else. To counteract your bully, your first step is to stop being a victim. You are in charge of your own attitude. You decide to be a winner or a loser. Choose winning. Remember, bullies pick their victims. If you stop acting like a victim, your big-footed bully boss will have to go elsewhere to satisfy his need for superiority.

Find Allies

Look for allies in this game. If the bully's victims stick together, they can shield each other. If you refuse to be coerced, you will not be pushed around. Stand your ground calmly and do your job without succumbing to undue pressure. You can win. In the end, it is the hammer, not the anvil that breaks.

Be an Asset

Make the most of whatever relationship you have with the boss. If you can find common aims, talk to him about them. Get him to see you as strong and goal focused. He won't want to cripple your spirit if he thinks you can help him to reach his goals.

Approach this monster gingerly. Make sure your tone is friendly and your complaints matter of fact. Simple, straightforward discussions about what needs to be done in the future may be productive. Long accusations about her past transgressions will certainly end in a new round of power plays. Amateur psychoanalysis is out for both of you.

Ask questions; do not issue ultimatums. Challenge the course of action or the decision, not this boss's authority. Once the discussion is over, summarize it in an e-mail to document any agreements you have reached. Keep a copy.

Stay consistently strong. If you succumb to threats and bullying part of the time, they will not go away.

Be Proactive

Learn to cut off tyrannical tactics before they occur. Be generous with information you want to share. Tell him about potential problems before you are asked. That way you will seem open and honest. If you seem to be hiding something, your boss will get even more suspicious and try to pry information out of you or bully you into admitting that you are a failure.

Avoid triggering the boss's temper. Figure out what sets her off. If she wants only good news, find a neutral way to communicate problems. Reports that are generated automatically are good for this, especially if they come from the group, rather than from individuals.

Control Your Emotions

One study found that 20 percent of bosses are bullies. Do these bosses want people to look up to them and think they can achieve that by looking down on everyone else? There are a number of reasons why a person might want to bully you, and none of them is pretty. Your Sasquatch supervisor may think he can climb to the top by stepping on you. If he never lets your light shine with the higher-ups in the organization, he can hog all the glory for your work. If he never asks your opinion, he may fear you will make him feel stupid. If he feels very afraid himself, of his inadequacies or of his boss, he may take it out on you by making you afraid of him. Maybe that's the only way he can feel powerful in the face of his own terrors.

First and foremost, do not lose your temper. Any insult is hard to take. Insults from the boss can be the most excruciating. No matter how personal they seem, remember that you are probably just a convenient victim, that the boss is just trying to vent his spleen, and that you just happened by.

Power players delight in raising an emotional reaction. Hang on to your emotions. Use a matter-of-fact tone and express your response with as much cool as you can muster. Suppose he says, "This quarterly analysis is totally incoherent. You are so stupid, I am surprised you can find your car in the parking lot three days out five."

You would naturally be sorely tempted to lash back with threats to drive that car into his backside. But, remember, he used those words to rile you. The best way to frustrate him is not get riled. Instead say, "I am certain that the figures in the report are correct. Which of the conclusions do you take issue with?" Keeping your temper in this emotionally charged situation will be difficult, but if you are ready in advance, you will have a better chance of staying on point. It will be worth the effort to know he failed, and you did not. Bullies do not keep dropping bombs if the bombs consistently fail to explode.

Stand up to rude behavior. In fact, you can take this advice to stand up to Bigfoot literally. Try this: when you see him coming toward your desk with his chin raised and his fists clenched, stand up and greet him warmly. Don't make a fist yourself. Just say as nicely as you can, "How can I help you?"

Put It in Writing

Do not cave in at the first sign of pressure from above. Dictators do not brook any resistance to their wishes. In the face of this, without insisting, press for your point of view. If she insists that you have to do it her way, tell her you would like some time to think it over. Then send her an e-mail with your rationale clearly laid out. Some bosses who cannot stand to be challenged in person will read and consider written arguments presented in an objective tone. And the written message will put you on record. If you are forced to do the task badly, you will have proof that it was not your decision that led to the breakdown.

Keep Your Boss on Track

Pick your fights. You cannot win every point. There are issues that are trivial to you that matter to the boss. Give in on those.

Watch out for tacky tactics. Your bully may claim that "top management" is putting on the pressure. This may be true, in which case you are both in the same boat and should act like fellow travelers. But sometimes this is a ploy. There are many such. Learn to recognize the ones your boss uses and to counter them. You can do this by just saying them out loud. "Perhaps, the VP doesn't understand the complexity of what we are dealing with. I am sure she doesn't want us to rush so much that we do shoddy work. If there is no time to do it right, we will have to take the time to do it over. That can't be what she wants."

If your boss stops paying attention when you are in the middle of saying something, offer to come back at a more convenient time. But do not go away without making a specific date. Then, when that time comes, you can remind her that the time was set aside for your discussion. Apply some pressure to get the attention you deserve.

Caveat: if you see a pattern of difficulty in getting people to hear you out, you may need to sharpen your communication skills. If you are longwinded or go into too much detail when you want people to listen, you may be encouraging them to lose interest. Be succinct. Make sure you make your side of the story appealing to the boss to encourage her to listen.

When to Surrender

Having a boss who steps on you is worse if you are someone who needs a lot of moral support. Your own personality will make the problem feel worse to you than it would to someone who is not so sensitive to what others think of him.

Also, if you are fearful of never finding another job, you will be overly intimidated by threats of being fired. How many times has your boss thundered about this one? How often has he actually fired someone? If his fulminations are a bluff, stop worrying about them. On the other hand, getting fired by this person may be a blessing. You will be able to collect unemployment while you activate your plan to find your next job.

One final course of action is to go to your boss—if you are sure it will not enrage him—and tell him that you need him to relate to you on a professional level. If you fear he will harm you physically if you stand up to him, find a way to keep your head down until you can activate your escape plan.

8

ABOMINABLE SNOWMAN
EGOMANIACAL AND INHUMANE

Also known as Yeti, this mythical giant lives in the Himalayas.
Though it shows up as benign in some movies, everyone who
believes in it is afraid of it.

Would it surprise you that people who believe in the Abominable Snowman think that he and Bigfoot are related? Bigfoot
abuses individuals with verbal attacks, criticizes employees in
front of other people, does everything she can to make her
people feel small and stunt their career growth. The Abominable Snowman applies these same heartless behaviors to
whole categories of people, applies the same moral self-cen-
teredness to rules of law and ethics, and the same self-serv-
ing attitudes to the entire planet. Some of these monsters
are purely despicable. They lie, steal, and take or give bribes.
They engage in insider trading, use dishonest accounting
practices, fix prices, and make and sell dangerous products.
    One product liability case involved a manufacturer of
camping equipment used by children. The indictment in
a criminal case against the company stated that they had
failed to fireproof their tents. The prosecution had copies of
memos indicating that the fireproofing would have cost one

dollar per tent. To save on production costs, the managers of the department, with the approval of their top management, decided to forego the fireproofing. To make one more dollar in profit! As a result, two young boys burned to death and another was severely disfigured.

This kind of heartlessness is inexplicable. It is bad enough when we hear about an individual who treats his fellow human beings with such disdain, but this took a group of people, who had to discuss the issue, to analyze its pros and cons, to look at spreadsheets telling them how their decision would affect the bottom line. They consciously decided to bet children's lives against profit. All too often these days, we hear managers explaining their actions purely on the basis of economic performance. Values and human decency do not seem to figure in their equations.

Some breeds of Abominable Snowmen hate anyone who is different from them. If you thought Bigfoot's snobbism was bad, here we are dealing with racists, sexists, and ageists. And then there are the snakes who will pollute the environment, produce dangerous products, lie, cheat, and steal to accomplish nothing more than putting a few dollars in their own pockets.

Astonishing as it is, these dastardly bosses find lots of employees willing to aid them in doing their dishonorable deeds. People go to work everyday knowing that the companies and the managers they serve are cheating, lying, and stealing. Employees let them get away with it. What have we come to? Are that many people completely lacking in morals? Well, sometimes the trouble just sneaks up on them.

The worst snakes in the grass are extraordinarily ego-driven and dedicated to their nefarious goals. They communicate a great focus of commitment. Ordinarily, managerial dedication is a powerful attraction for employees. We are drawn to leaders by their devotion to a cause or an idea. With some bosses, however, we find out later that their dedication has a dark side, that they are willing to use immoral means to achieve their ends. The power they amass creates even more of the arrogance that fuels their diseased ambition. They will break the law, and they will invent vile and underhanded tactics against which no law has yet been passed.

This disregard for their fellow human beings, of course, extends to the people who work for them. Frequently, these managers also see their employees as pawns rather than people. Do not expect them to protect the health and well-being of their staff anymore than they do that of their customers.

Good managers are hard on problems, but soft on people. Managers who behave like Abominable Snowmen are hard on everyone, hard as ice. They think nothing of subjecting their employees to harm. At their best, they are unfeeling. At their worst, they are sociopaths who take pleasure in inflicting pain on other people.

Corporate Reality

A moral turpitude seems to pervade quite a lot of workplaces. When people stuck in such places wake up to what's going on around them, they feel disgusted and dirty by association. Yet, there is seldom a clear path to fixing the situation.

The arrogance of power leads some business people to cut corners, fudge safety reports, and double-deal with their suppliers and their employees. Many people get sucked into doing things that are immoral, illegal, or unethical for long periods of time, and they often find themselves hard pressed to get out. Their children depend on the money they make. They have a big mortgage. Or maybe, following their Abominable Bossman, they have broken the law themselves. It reminds one of some character in *The Sopranos* who wants to get out of the mob but would be murdered by his brother crooks if he tried.

How do people get roped into collusion with these abominations? For one thing, the bosses they follow to perdition can wield a lot of power. They are so focused, so motivated that we find their dedication to success irresistible. We admire their swagger. Somehow we miss that all that confidence is a cover for lying, cheating, selling defective products, and flouting the rules, with self-aggrandizement as the end.

Or maybe we just glide down a slippery slide oiled with small concessions to pragmatic solutions. We shave a little off our conscience here, a tiny, tiny bit there, a sliver today, a bit of a bigger chunk tomorrow, until the voice of Jiminy Cricket is drowned out completely. The next thing we know, we are standing by and watching our bosses commit indictable offenses. Or, far worse, we actively help them.

Even if you don't go up the river, you probably won't go up the ladder, either. Foul bosses stunt the careers of their employees. Where immoral bosses are in power, eventually the whole organization suffers. The company gets caught. Consumers shun the shoddy products. Lawsuits to redress damage done to people or the environment sap the company's assets. Where immoral bosses are in power, people start to guard what they say and restrict what they do. Productivity and innovation suffer from lack of cooperation and information exchange. Hostility and suspicion reign.

Strategies for Coping with Abominable Behavior

Even if you are not the direct victim of a scoundrel boss, when you know your boss has no morals, you know you can be next. The conflict between the way you have to live at work and your values leads to great internal stress. Eventually, you begin to mistrust everything the boss says or does. Your position becomes intolerable.

That's what happened to Barbara Sanford when she got a new boss.

Barbara worked for twelve years in the corporate communications department of a pharmaceutical company. When
Chris arrived to take over her department, Barbara was editor in charge of employee communication, which included
an employee information Web site and a quarterly employee
magazine. Because she had such a high-visibility job, she
knew hundreds of people in the company, including all of
the members of the executive committee. People liked her
and her work. On the Web site, she liked to keep a balance
between news of weddings, births, and service anniversaries
and hard news about profits, new products, reorganizations,
and the like. She loved her job, and unlike her colleague
Earl, she had no resentment about Chris being brought in
from the outside to manage the department.

Barbara never expected any serious changes in what she
was doing. But from day one, Chris seemed to have it in for
her. He immediately announced what he saw as his mission:
total modernization of the department. "Management has
brought me in here," he said at his first staff meeting, "to
make this the kind of corporation communications department that can serve the future of the company, not the past.
I am putting all of you on notice that what you are doing now
is automatically suspect. We are going to bring this department into the twenty-first century, even though many of you
are leftovers from the last millennium."

Barbara was not as frightened by the pronouncement as
the others. She had moved their old monthly print magazine
to the Web. She kept the quarterly magazine for the older
employees and the retirees. Otherwise, her efforts were right
in line with what she knew the most up-to-date people in her
profession were doing at their companies. She did not imagine that Chris's ultimatum would mean much to her.

Chris's next move puzzled Barbara at first. He asked her
to do a cost and quality evaluation comparing their present
printer with one in another state. She protested that working

with a local printer was much more efficient than trying to work with one so far away. "We have done business with these local people for many years."

"That's exactly the kind of thinking we want to stop," Chris said. Since he insisted, she complied. Her study showed that cost would be a little lower with the new printer, but quality was about equal. In her final recommendation, she suggested that the cost savings would be negligible—around $500 a year—not enough to take the business away from a longtime local supplier who relied on their business.

"This is small town," she told Chris, "and many of our employees know the people who work at the printer's. We have a good reputation for being community oriented. Do we really want to risk upsetting that to save a few hundred dollars?"

"Spare me the small-town thinking," Chris said. "This company may have been a country club for years, but these are hardheaded times. If you can't be profit minded, you have no business working in a profit-making organization."

"Suppose I just ask the local company to give us a break on the price. I am sure they will do that to keep the business."

"I am not here to mollycoddle them and teach them how to be competitive." At his insistence, they switched to the other printer.

Barbara complained about the decision to her friend Paul, who asked her a question that stopped her mind. "There are printers all over the place. If lower price was what he wanted, why did he have you survey just ours and one other? What is so special about this printer in Cincinnati?"

"Why didn't I think of that," she wondered. "We can't change now. We just signed a one-year contract. I have been so busy trying to look competent and cooperative, that I seem to be losing my strategic brain cells."

Paul's question haunted Barbara. Why the printer in Cincinnati? She kept thinking that Chris had an ulterior motive.

The idea of a kickback entered her mind fleetingly, but she dismissed it.

A couple of months later, Chris insisted that they call in a Web design firm to redesign the employee Web site. "Everyone likes it. It functions well," she said. "Our own IT people worked on it. Everyone thinks they did an excellent job."

"Web sites aren't cupcakes. Homemade is not necessarily better," Chris said.

Barbara was so conflicted about what Chris might be up to, she was afraid to challenge him. She got the proposal from the firm Chris wanted in Indianapolis. She made a half-hearted attempt to get him not to make the change. He resisted, and she capitulated.

"He was so intent on saving five hundred dollars on the magazine printing," she told Paul. "Now he is squandering tens of thousands on a new design we really don't need. But I don't have the nerve to remind him of what he told me about profit making."

Then, on the first Friday in May, Barbara got a call from the letter shop that mailed the magazine saying that the spring issue weighed more than usual. They needed authorization to spend the extra money on postage. Chris had strictly forbidden her to authorize overbudget expenses without his approval, and Chris was not in the office that day. His cell phone didn't answer, so she called his home number. A housekeeper answered and told her that Chris and his wife had left already for the weekend; gratuitously she added that they were probably in flight to Chris's niece's wedding in Cincinnati. Barbara had to go to Chris's boss the VP of PR for authorization of the extra postage.

Then she called Paul. Over a beer after work that evening, she told Paul that she could not get it out of her head that Chris was getting kickbacks. She wanted to do something, but she was not sure what. "At the very least, he is probably giving the business to his relatives and friends."

"But you don't know for sure," Paul said. "I would be careful. He's slick. He is not going to take kindly to accusations, even if they are veiled." Paul reminded her that she loved her job, and that Chris could move against her if she threatened him.

"I do love my job. At least I used to before he came along. I don't think it would be easy to get another like it. I guess I have to make the best of it. It frosts me though."

Barbara decided to say something innocuous to see how Chris would react. On Monday, she mentioned that she had had to call Chris at home for the postage authorization. She tried to keep her tone as lighthearted as she could muster. "Your housekeeper told me you went to a wedding in Cincinnati. If I had known I would have given you some stuff to drop off with the printer."

She watched his eyes as he looked into hers. She saw a look of recognition. She was more convinced than ever that Chris was up to nepotism at the very least.

For the next couple of months, Barbara did her job and tried to steer clear of Chris. Her job anxiety levels went up when Chris fired her colleague Earl. The only good thing about that was that he was so busy interviewing for Earl's replacement that he had little time to scrutinize her work.

The winner in the hunt for a new public relations manager turned out not to be Earl's assistant manager, Bob, as everyone had hoped. Chris brought in someone from the outside, a former associate. People in the department were disappointed. Barbara's suspicions grew.

"Those people scare me, Paul," she said over lunch one day. "And this Larry, who took Earl's place, is a super sleaze. He calls me "Babe." I cannot bear it. Chris gave him a company car to use until he gets settled. He came here from a hundred miles away, for heaven's sake. What is he talking about 'gets settled'? The two of them are constantly taking each other out to fancy lunches. I know they are using their expense accounts. And Larry keeps bragging about how he can help me liaison with the new Web designer. I know they are up to no good."

The following week Chris asked her to do a feature on Larry for the next magazine issue. "I think it would be good to introduce him to the company. Build his reputation and that of our department."

Barbara objected. "We have always made it policy never to use our public relations skills and outlets for ourselves in this department," she said. "Besides we already have a feature for that issue on the launch of Praximum. We always give precedence to new product launch information."

The meeting went on for an hour. Despite Barbara's arguments, Chris insisted on the article about Larry. In the end he questioned her professionalism and her loyalty.

"I am loyal to the company and my own values," she finally burst out. "I have no loyalty to you and your cronies." Barbara shocked herself with her outburst. She was even more surprised when Chris reneged.

"Forget about this for now," he said. "We will work this out another way."

At performance appraisal time Chris dropped his bomb. He gave her a "Meets No Expectations" rating. For the first time in her twelve years at the firm, she did not get a raise. He cited a delay in completing the new Web site and increased costs for the summer employee outing. She had perfectly logical reasons for all his issues, including some foot dragging by his Web consultants. He refused to change anything on the appraisal. The rules called for her to sign the form. She refused.

Again she went to Paul for advice and solace. "I am not going let him push me out so he can bring in another one of his vassals to help him steal from the company." There was fight in her voice, but there were tears in her eyes.

Chris did not give Barbara a chance to make a battle plan. The very next day he told her he was bringing in an "independent" firm to make an "objective" analysis of the quality of her group's work. "I expect you to give them your full cooperation," he said. "Anything less will be grounds for me to fire you."

Barbara knew for some time that her job was in jeopardy. Still, it was a shock to hear it right from Chris's mouth. Her one objective over the next weeks was to make sure he did not take her job away from her. After months of trying to get along on her own, she played her trump card. She went to Mike, the Admin VP who was Chris's boss. She was going over Chris's head, but she had known Mike for years. She did not tell him about her suspicions about kickbacks, nor did she say she thought someone should audit Chris's expense account. She did not even mention Chris's threats about firing her. All she told him were the facts about her assignments and her performance appraisal. "Mike, I hate to put you on the spot." she said. "I know you cannot reveal anything to me, and I do not want you to. All I ask is that you look into what he is doing and the decisions he makes. He does not know that I have come to you. And I don't expect you to tell me anything about what you find. I will just go back to my desk and do my job the best way I can. I will cooperate with the consultant who is going to evaluate me."

After that meeting with Mike everything seemed to stop. Months went by and nothing changed. She knew that the evaluation consultant had finished his report, but she never heard anything of the results. She was in limbo, and she hated it, but she waited it out.

Then, shortly after the beginning of the year, Larry suddenly left the company. Less than two weeks later, Chris said that he would be leaving too, as soon as they found a replacement for him. He said that he and Larry had decided to go into business for themselves.

Barbara never found out what had happened behind the scenes. She and Paul speculated about why Chris left so abruptly, but they never found out for sure. As is frequently the case with dishonest employees, no announcements were made.

This is the difficulty with combating a snake in the grass. If your abominable boss is at all good at the game, you will never find the smoking gun. Without the proof, your motives may be suspect. Upper management may not see events from your perspective. You could come out of such a situation with your conscience, but not your job, intact.

Your moral choices are your own to make. Examine your suspicions. Do not overreact before you have proof. Grandstand plays in which you prematurely expose your boss's vices and transgressions could backfire on you.

Stay Above the Fray

If you feel sure that something wrong is afoot in your organization, do all you can to make things right. At the very least, keep clean yourself. Withstand the temptations an immoral or amoral boss dangles. To stand against immoral management takes enormous courage, but you must try to marshal it. Regardless of what they offer, guard yourself from falling into the prevailing moral turpitude. Live your business life by your values and your humanity.

How can you avoid falling into the trap? Learn to identify and avoid bosses who have lost their ability to distinguish right from wrong. Watch for the telltale signs of a snake in the grass. One of the first indications is the boss who dismisses any negative information, who brooks no discussion of the merits of a course of action. Fine points of moral judgment are not usually the first considerations to emerge when businesspeople try to solve a problem or decide a course of action. Costs, profitability, time constraints, available resources, avoiding unwanted collateral effects, these things come up first. That's normal. But if other considerations are suppressed, if your boss always wants a fast, facile solution and cuts off any discussion of the moral or ethical merits of the decision, you had better keep on guard.

Watch for Secretiveness

Any organization has a right to keep its proprietary business practices a secret. New product development and research are usually closely held. Fine. But if your company is burying the results of safety testing of its products, you know something's fishy. All those dreadful stories in the press about how companies hid information about the dangerous side effects of pharmaceutical products did not happen without the cooperation of a lot of very smart people. Where were their consciences? Did anyone around the conference room table bother to say, "I think we are on thin moral ice here?" Out of the thousands who worked at Enron, one or two people pressed for sanity. How many people in cigarette companies have been involved in hiding the evidence that has led to their having to pay out billions in class-action judgments? Mass insanity is alive and well and living in some of our best-known corporations. If your company is keeping secrets about harmful practices, you are in deep trouble.

On the other hand, bosses who protest their morality too loudly deserve a second look. Honest people rarely go around declaring that they are not crooks.

Then there are the sanctimonious hypocrites who accuse anyone who questions their motives of a lack of objectivity. Too much objectivity and you find yourself treating people— be they employees, customers, or the people who live around the polluting plant—as "objects."

You can destroy your own reputation by allying yourself with scoundrels. I have known a couple of people who were corrupted by the roles they were asked to play. Both were brilliant young men who were adopted by powerful mentors who sought to use them and promised to reward them. They were both put to work as hatchet men, sent into areas of the organization to fire people or act as front men for bosses who did not want to be identified with unpopular programs.

JIM'S STORY

Jim Bellamy admired his tough-guy department head in the marketing department of an automobile company. His boss repeatedly put him in charge of problem areas and encouraged him to work fast to get projects on track. Often at his boss's suggestion and always with his approval, Jim used brutal methods. He bullied people in public, fired some on the spot, and browbeat the survivors into submission. Soon, fear preceded Jim's arrival in any new assignment. After a while, even if he wanted to change his style, he would have had difficulty. People would have thought the "new Jim" was just another one of his stratagems. Experience had taught everyone in the department that he was a cold-blooded executioner and to greet him with fear and suspicion.

Jim has been lucky so far. His mentor remains in power, and he still has a job. But they preside over a less and less successful organization. If you ask other people in the industry, all the best people have already left the company. The interesting thing is that people hate Jim, not his boss, who is the real demon.

MORT'S STORY

Mort Holler was put to work orchestrating the first major staff reduction in an insurance company. Mort's boss gave him the assignment, but he laid down the rules, and they were harsh, especially for an organization that had no experience of large layoffs. Mort worked behind the scenes for three months, and then he fired sixty middle managers in three days.

From time to time all organizations must let people go. The objection to Mort's project was not its ends but its means. He drew up a list of those marked for what business people call, with remarkable candor, termination. One by one, the "chosen" were called into their boss's office. Their bosses were given no choice but to do the deed Mort's way. Their bosses had to give them the bad news and then send them directly to an outplacement firm for processing. The fired employees were forbidden to return to their desks to get their belongings or say good-bye to their coworkers.

Mangers all over the company did the dirty deeds, but Mort was known as the architect of the effort. He had been so focused on the project that he never contemplated the next step. Shortly afterward, his boss fired him. When it happened he finally saw the light. What else could have been the outcome? He was a man now universally despised in the company. How could he ever recover his reputation? What function could he possibly perform when no one in the organization wanted to work with him? Again he took the fall for the big boss who was behind the scenes pulling his strings.

He tried to find another job in the industry, but word had gone out, and other companies shunned him, even in other parts of the country. After two and half years of unemployment, he started a restaurant that lasted less than a year. He was drinking more and more and had a hard time staying on his toes. Eventually alcoholism took over. Not even his friends who stood by him in the dark days after the purge know where he is now.

Employees are attracted to powerful people and hope for a chance to share in their glory. The trouble with serving the dastardly is that you could very likely wind up one of their victims.

See It for What It Is

Ordinarily, with other types of monster bosses, it's helpful to figure out what motivates your boss's monstrous behavior. With the law-breaking boss, however, it's fairly easy to see that most of the time we are looking at naked greed for money or power. You may be facing some advanced form of megalomania. Whatever it is, knowing the cause will not give you a clue to solving the problem.

Assess Alternatives

Carefully evaluate the alternatives, not only yours, but theirs. Resist the temptation to fight fire with fire. If you combat your boss's subterfuges with your own dirty tricks, you will become tainted yourself. Playing their game by their rules means turning into one of them. Instead, try to influence the boss or the decision-making process whenever you suspect moral issues are being ignored. Pose questions that will direct attention to ethics. Your attempts may be ignored, but at least you will have tried to push things in the direction of good.

Draw the Line

Look to your own power. You have more than you think. Abominable bosses can almost never do their dastardly deeds without the cooperation of their staff. To do her job effectively, your boss needs you. It is likely she can be severely hurt if you refuse to cooperate. Don't threaten her. Just draw the line on what you will and will not do. True, you may risk being tossed out. But if she fires you, she will have no way of controlling what you know about what she is doing, so she probably won't fire you if you know too much. Besides, finding a new job can often be less trouble than keeping the one you have.

If you suspect the boss's motives, question them. Use your supportive communication techniques. Do not begin with confrontation. Just ask, "I need to understand why we are doing this."

Shine a Light

Call the game. Unscrupulous behavior is like the emperor's nakedness. Everyone can comfortably pretend it is not there. Sometimes people delude themselves into thinking they are fooling all the people all of the time. But they have to give up their tricky tactics if someone calls attention to them. This can work even if you seem to be joking when you bring up the subject, as in, "Gee, Howie, if I didn't know you so well, I might think you were ignoring standard accounting practices with this report."

It might work. At the very least it will put the boss on notice that his slip is showing.

If your company has promulgated a value system, use it. The principles by which you all work should be more than a sign posted in the lobby or a page on the corporate Web site. You can point to those glowing words and try to get the people around you to live by them.

Do not let your own conscience fall asleep on the job. You cannot accept "I was just following orders" as an excuse for yourself. This can become extremely difficult, especially if your wayward boss tries to entice your cooperation with money, status, and power aimed at blurring your judgment.

Be Thorough

If you are already involved in such a quagmire, you need to stop, analyze carefully, and assess your alternatives. Think it through. How bad is the situation? Are you in danger of turning a blind eye to real mendacity? Or could you be over-reacting with scrupulous morality? Once you are sure you are not imaging things, your main goal should be to keep your conscience alive. Draw a line that you are not willing to cross. Try to influence the organization. Bring up the issues that concern you. There should be nothing wrong with your saying, "I am wondering if we are not taking too much of a risk by not coming clean with the design flaws in this model and just recalling it. We will suffer short-term losses, but in the long run, the right thing ethically may be the best business decision."

That kind of sally should get an enthusiastic response from all but the most hardened criminals. Your boss may not agree, but she should take your concerns seriously. If your questions get discussed and settled, fine. If they are dismissed out of hand, you are on very shaky ground with this boss. The worst response would be for her to question your loyalty. A person who raises loyalty as an issue in the face of a moral dilemma is asking if you are willing to shut your conscience up for the sake of "team spirit."

Document Everything

However, if your boss becomes irate or accuses you of disloyalty, do not become confrontational. Document your own behavior and the boss's response. And then extricate yourself—as quickly as you can. If your boss is truly abominable and committing a felony, you might consider a visit to your state attorney general. That would be a big step, but whistle-blowing may be the only truly moral response to the harm that is being done.

When to Surrender

Beware the person who reaches for the first expedient and manipulates people and situations to gain power. And remember, whatever she will do to other people, she may eventually do to you.

Even if your own sense of morality wouldn't stop you from going along with the dastardly intentions of your favorite scoundrel, maybe you should think twice about it as a matter of self-interest. If the world at large cannot trust him, neither can you. If she will flout environmental laws, put employees' or customers' lives in danger, or play dirty tricks on the competition, what makes you think she will be fair and honorable in her dealings with you?

Remember that your reputation as well as your conscience is on the line. At the very least you may wind up with a company name on your resume that turns all future employers against you as a job candidate. Or you may wind up going to jail with your boss—or, considering what a clever snake he is, instead of him. If common human decency doesn't keep you from helping your boss screw the planet or endanger innocent people, maybe you will want to be good in order to save your own hide. You do not want to be interviewing for your next job and have to field questions about what you knew about your previous employer's lawlessness and when you knew it.

Find another job—fast!

9

LOCH NESS MONSTER
NEVER THERE, NO DIRECTION

The legend of a monstrously large sea serpent living in the deep, dark waters of Loch Ness, a lake in Scotland, goes back 1,500 years. Reputable people claim to have seen "Nessie." Believers also offer fuzzy photos and suggestive sonar readings but no incontrovertible evidence. From the PBS program *Nova* to crackpot Web sites, the debate rages: Is this primeval beast a fairytale, or does it really exist?

As Erich Nilsson walked the long, gleaming parquet hallway toward the corporate boardroom, he told himself he didn't care what happened at the meeting. In his hand, the notes for his presentation were soaking up the sweat from his palm. He had barely ever been in this poshest area of the headquarters building. He had little idea who was going to be at this meeting and no notion at all of what interested them. Clutching the disk containing his PowerPoint presentation, he mentally reviewed his four major points about the successes of his quality-assurance team. But doubts and ignorance had shredded whatever confidence he might have been able to muster.

Erich had talked over his presentation outline with his wife. He had even asked his mother-in-law about what he should include. The one person who had the information to enlighten him on how to succeed at this meeting was his boss—George. But Erich had never gotten to ask George even one question during the last ten, tense days of preparation.

A little over a week before, George had sent an e-mail telling Erich he "was expected" to present at this "important meeting." It gave the time and the place and ended with George's favorite expression. "I know I can count on you." That was George's entire concept of management.

After getting the e-mail, Erich had seen George exactly once—during the biweekly staff meeting. Erich had hardly paid attention to the discussion that day, so focused was he on getting to George as soon as the meeting ended so he could ask about the presentation in the boardroom. Speaking before any group made Erich nervous. Just going to the boardroom made him antsy. Not knowing what his presentation was supposed to accomplish absolutely terrified him. If he could corner George, he could at least find out who would attend the meeting and what they wanted to hear about. But then, just as the staff got to the last agenda item, George pulled one of his cute disappearing acts. He announced that he was leaving the last topic—the coordination of the budget process—in Erich's capable hands. With a warm, winning smile—that smile that had convinced Erich at his interview for this job that George would be the best of all possible bosses—with that same smile, George had said, "Erich, why don't you take over this meeting now?" It hadn't really been a question. Before Erich could move out of his seat to the head of the table, George was out the door.

Repeated e-mails, visits to George's office, and phone messages left on his voice mail and cell phone yielded no response—no insight, no encouragement. Abandoned by George again, Erich felt as if he worked for an empty chair.

Erich's guts twisted as he turned the knob on the boardroom door.

Identifying Loch Ness Behavior

At their worst, absentee bosses leave their employees without clear goals, guidance, leadership, or information. On their own, orphaned workers flounder, take all the chances. Sometimes, as a consequence, they fail.

What keeps the Loch Ness Monster 812 feet down at the bottom of that lake? How much sonar and underwater stroboscopic camera equipment does an employee need to keep handy to try to locate, or even prove the existence of the boss who is never there when you need him?

Let's start with a list of the possible reasons why bosses make themselves scarce.

Geography is a likely excuse. If you are running the Mendocino office and your boss works out of Chicago, that's one whole category of problems. In many global corporations, people manage or are managed by people they have never met. If you never see your boss because he is hundreds or thousands of miles away, that is one kind of problem.

However, if you and your boss occupy the same building, complex, town, or even state, you have to figure out why your boss keeps away from you. Some reasons may be understandable or even forgivable, but others may be nefarious. Here are a few possibilities:

- Is your boss completely ignorant about what you do? It could be too intimidating for him to try to manage you if you are the department expert in statistical analysis and he barely passed statistics in college. This will be especially true if you use phrases like "two deviations above the mean" when you talk to him.
- Is your boss afraid you are smarter than he is? If you are smarter, that's fine, but if that scares the boss, it would keep him away.
- Is your boss so completely overwhelmed by what he has to do that he cannot find time for anything else?

- Is she so shy she rarely interacts with anyone?
- Is he a snob who thinks talking to someone at your level is beneath him? Does he have such a sense of his own importance that he feels he cannot spare the time from his really important matters to pay attention to what you do?
- Or is she just clueless, stupid, or so ignorant about her job that she doesn't see the need to involve herself in the work of her people?
- Is there something nefarious in the fact that your boss is not around most of the time? "Elusive" can mean deceptive or deceitful.

Obviously there can be a number of reasons your boss would avoid you and your situation: He sees failure in the future and wants to distance himself. Or perhaps he knows your group is going to be eliminated or your division sold off. Maybe he is spending his time with others who report to him as a way of keeping his job when the axe falls. We could come up with lots of these reasons, but you get my drift.

Corporate Reality

Many corporations have cut their staffs to the bone. Your boss may now be doing the job that two or three managers used to do, or she may be expected to manage and do a lot of technical or administrative work, too. How pressed for time is she? You may see her as a Loch Ness Monster, but if she is working for Dracula, she may just not have time or energy left for the demands of her management job.

Strategies for Coping with Loch Ness Behavior

For the legend to stay alive, the Loch Ness Monster has to surface every once in a while. So it is with your elusive boss. She may seem like an optical illusion, but she has to put in an appearance some time, and when she does, if you are going to right this situation, you have to be ready. If you work for a phantom manager, the first thing you need is a way to attract her attention.

If It's Geography

If you think geography is the issue, let's ask another question first: Do you and your boss have a decent working relationship? Consider this: If you have a boss who for one of the other reasons mentioned above prefers not to talk to you, he can hide behind the geography. If the problem is primarily geography, dealing with it should be pretty straightforward. Your first objective should be establishing a work routine that will bring you and your boss into a closer professional relationship despite the fact that she lives in another city or state or even on another continent.

Take the Initiative

If at all possible you and your boss need to be in the same place at the same time to do this. Take the initiative. Set up a "team-building" meeting for the two of you. If you fear that he will not respond to your invitation for a one-to-one, try setting up a broader meeting with the boss in attendance. One way or another you have to psych out what will get the two of you into the same room at the same time for a discussion.

There are a few ways to manage this. A lot of how you do it depends on how far you or the boss would have to travel. If you are in Bangalore and your boss is in Chicago, maybe a phone conference is the best you will be able to arrange. Or if there is any time during the year that you both have to be in the same place at the same time, suggest that the two of you arrive early or stay a bit later so you can have time together. If the distance is not so daunting, can you arrange to travel to where the boss is? Do not assume the boss will say no to your request for the travel. Ask anyway.

Whether it's in person or on the telephone, ask for a meeting and specify that you need it to set goals and objectives for yourself, or your team if you are supervisor or manager yourself. If you say, "I need to talk to you. I think we have a problem," you are going to sound as if you are inviting your manager to a wake. You want to get the boss to say yes if that's at all possible, so make the idea sound attractive.

If you try for a face-to-face and get turned down, or if the geography precludes it, try to schedule a regular telephone conference.

Lay a Foundation

Your goal for the first meeting (or phone conference) is not to tell the boss everything you have ever wanted to say or to ask every question that has been left hanging. You have only one objective and that is for the boss to leave the meeting feeling it was comfortable and productive—*for him.* So restrict the agenda for your first effort to one that will yield results he will value. Yes, yes, your aims and your feelings are important too, but keep your eyes on the prize. You are trying to establish a relationship the boss will want to continue. Look at this meeting as the first step on your way to getting the attention you warrant. If you can get the boss to look forward to the next meeting, you can use that next encounter to start work on your own needs.

Build Trust

At that next meeting, cement the trust between you and your boss, and lay out a more or less formal process and schedule of communications between you. Fix it so that future meetings will become routine and regular, even if those "meetings" take place in cyberspace or on the telephone. At that point, your geography problem will be solved.

Take your time. Get to your goal by making each step along the way worth the boss's while. You have read this several times so far in this book. I cannot overemphasize the importance of this, though. If you want your boss to do the things that motivate you, you are going to have to motivate her.

If Your Boss Avoids You

Much more difficult would be the boss who actively stays away from you. It may seem daunting to psych out a person you never see, but you have to try to see through those murky waters. Let's figure out your boss. Why is he not there for you? Let me give you a few neutral ways of thinking about it. In my experience, there are only a few basic reasons people in general do not do what they should do at work:

- They don't even realize it's required.
- There is no reward for doing it.
- There is no punishment for not doing it.
- They don't know how to do it, but they would if they learned how.
- They know how, but the task is somehow so unpleasant or difficult that they find it punishing to do it.
- They couldn't do it or learn it no matter how hard they tried.

If we take these issues in turn, I think we can go a long way toward figuring out what's up with your elusive boss.

Probably the hardest one of these for you to believe is the first one—that she doesn't know that she has a responsibility to keep you informed, to give you that support you need to function in your job, to make sure you have the performance feedback you need to keep motivated and to improve.

After the years I spent training managers, it would not surprise me at all if your boss was put in charge without being given the least indication of what was expected of her.

Almost no one gets management training anymore. Besides, there may be some other problems about how your manager assumed her position.

ROSEMARY'S STORY

Rosemary Potter had a lot of trouble when she took her first supervisory position. Rosemary had been one of a group of account analysts in a big packaged-goods company. She was relatively new in the job, there only two years, when Roger, her department manager, tapped her to be group head. He picked Rosemary because she had a master's degree in economics. Not that that had anything at all to do with how good or not she would be as a boss. But Roger lacked an advanced degree, and he was impressed with Rosemary's. Rosemary's coworkers all had more experience than she, and they knew what they were doing, so Roger thought, "Why not?" He had a rationale for the decision, and that's all Roger ever needed to get rid of another pesky choice he had to make. He made the announcement and forgot about it.

However, the news shocked Rosemary and her coworkers. Ed had been sure he would get the job since he had seniority—not necessarily a reasonable expectation, but one he harbored nonetheless. Although Nance and Haley had been pretty close friends with Rosemary, they both also had more experience than she did, and they felt slighted when she was promoted over them.

For her part, Rosemary sensed the resentment and puzzlement of her new subordinates. She didn't feel she had any right to manage them. She was loath to assert any authority over her former teammates. A shy and bookish person by nature, she had fully expected that Ed, who had trained her when she arrived, would be her new boss. Now she was his. So she hid out in her new corner office, made herself scarce when there was a decision to be made, and told herself that the people in the department knew what they were doing and did not need her to interfere.

To be honest, Rosemary was intimidated, especially since, as soon as her appointment was announced, her former teammates started treating her strangely. Ed, who had always taken a big brotherly attitude toward her, became openly hostile. Nance and Haley stopped inviting her to go to lunch with them. Rosemary began to resent their reaction.

Can you see the dynamics? Rosemary's story, and many very like it, are lived out in corporations every day. No one told Rosemary what to do as a manager. No one helped her overcome the difficulties of the transition from coworker to boss. And so her reaction was just to keep her head down and hope for the best.

Is that what your boss is doing? If so, you need a strategy to deal with that. Is your situation complicated by the fact that you resented his appointment in the first place?

If this is the case, take some straightforward steps to get both of you over this hump. Stop fantasizing that your Loch Ness Monster will get hit by a bus (or I guess I should say a speedboat), or that the big boss will come to his senses and fire your boss and give you her job. If you are unable to overcome this resentment, maybe it's time to leave. Remember what we said in Chapter 3—hopeless is hopeless. There is no future in sticking with a miserable situation if you cannot fix it.

If Your Boss Is Underqualified

If your boss is avoiding you because she doesn't know what she should be doing—or is so intimidated by the job that she cannot bring herself to actually do it, you can start by having a reassuring meeting with her. Your objective is for her to come out of the meeting feeling that you are on her side. If your boss is isolating himself because he feels circumstances have isolated him, that's all you want to accomplish as a first step. Do not get overly ambitious. For example, say: "Mary, I want to update you on how things are going with the Zorn Project. I think there is some good progress with it, and you might want to pass it along to Mike at your next staff meeting."

She might say, "Why don't you just send Mike an e-mail." It will be up to you to convince her that talking with you will be painless. Then do everything you can to make it so.

At the second meeting—not too soon, but do not wait too long either—say, the next week—when you ask for some more of her time, be ready to start gradually making these meetings more about what you need. In a few weeks, you will be on your way to being managed in the way you need to be.

This is the process with any elusive boss who avoids you because of his ignorance or back-burner feelings of inadequacy. If your boss avoids you because he is arrogant, we face a more difficult problem.

If Your Boss Is Arrogant

If your evasive boss thinks what you do is beneath his notice, or if he is too busy kissing up to the higher-ups to have time for you, we have to look at working around the situation, not fixing it.

Bob McGrath worked for Phil Mackey, the top account executive at a major Atlanta public relations firm. Like his coworkers, Bob had learned his job by fire, osmosis, and going on pure guts, working his way up from assistant account executive to account supervisor. Bob's focus was on his next promotion, which would be to account manager, and after that, he would be in line to become an account executive and get a chance at making some real money. Bob was hot to trot.

When he first started at the firm as a newly minted college grad with a degree in corporate communication, Bob did not care that the firm lacked a formal training program. Solving problems on his own challenged and energized him, and he could count on his colleague Lily, the account manager on the team, to help and to offer wisdom. Then one day Phil announced that Lily had made AE. He promoted Bob to account manger that same day. Yippee! Except that Phil disappeared almost completely once he announced the two promotions.

Phil was out there—bringing in business, traveling to visit clients, wining and dining them, gossiping on the telephone with people who could give him good contacts. Some bosses are two-faced. Phil had only one face, and it was perpetually turned toward the source of money. Certainly no AE at the firm would hold on to his job long, much less make a six-figure income at it, if he did not spend most of his time wooing clients to get contracts. The problem was that Phil never talked to Bob about anything at all except to say the equivalent of "Here's another job to do."

Bob went to Lily in her swanky new office and complained to her. "Look," she said, "when I had your job, I just handled things for Phil. You are good. Don't rock his boat and you'll be fine."

Don't rock his boat? All Bob wanted was enough information to do his work properly.

Bob had always thought Phil was a really cool guy. Now he considered Phil totally cold—a snob interested only in his own personal aggrandizement, who thought he was too good to bother with the people in the trenches. What bothered Bob most was that Phil treated him like an appliance—a function that could deliver on what Phil promised—but not as a person.

And that was another thing: those promises. Phil offered the clients services that were practically impossible to deliver. He never asked Bob whether a press release could be written, vetted, and delivered into the hands of twenty different key business news reporters in less than a day. If that's what he thought would impress the client, that's what he promised.

Then he took out the old BlackBerry and e-mailed Bob, telling him what needed to be done. And while Bob and his new, totally green assistant killed themselves to get the job done, Phil took the client to some fancy restaurant and drank overpriced wine.

There were times when Bob fantasized about letting the ball drop—not actually accomplishing the miracles Phil promised. But Bob knew what that would mean: Phil would fire him.

How would you estimate Bob's chances of reforming Phil—getting him to give Bob the attention he needed and the support he longed to have? I would say slim to nonexistent. I never got a chance to ask Phil the question, but I would bet the ranch that Phil would say, "Look, I had it worse than Bob. Trial by fire—that's how you learn this business."

Tossing a person into the deep end of the lake is certainly not the only way, much less the best way, to teach a person to swim. People do drown. And employees do fail, and lose clients for firms like Phil's. On the other hand, Phil knew he wasn't taking any big chances with the success of his team by loading the full responsibility on Bob. Phil must have had a pretty good idea that Bob could and would handle everything thrown at him.

Accentuate the Positive

With some sage counseling and soul searching, Bob finally came to understand what you may now need to absorb: If you work for a person like Phil, you can let the weight of responsibility crush you or you can take it as a compliment and an opportunity. Trial by fire may scare you, but think about all the heroes who defeated the bad guys in every monster movie you have ever seen. When the Martians landed, if Tom Cruise had gone to lunch and blubbered to his friends instead of standing up to the beasts, would anyone have wanted to watch the movie? What makes life, as well as movies, interesting is people standing up to situations and triumphing over them. Real heroes always have to go through the crucible to win their laurels. Be your own hero. Take the ball and run with it. Step up to the challenges. What other choice do you have?

Weigh Your Options

You can either leave your job now and find a more benign environment, or you can stay where you are, shoulder the responsibility, and learn not to let it grind you down.

Leaving his job was certainly an option for Bob, but he had to decide if he really wanted to move from the top to a lesser agency? Perhaps. Coming from his company, a smaller agency might move him up a lot faster than he would have moved—even on the fast track—where he was. If a supportive atmosphere was critical to him, he might work better and be more creative in a place where he did not feel so underappreciated. It might take him a few months to make the transition, but that could be okay. Having made up his mind to move, he would be better able to bear the stress knowing he was a short-timer.

The downside risk was that he might not be working with the big, important clients he was used to. The work might bore him. His learning curve could drop off.

This is a very personal call. A bad work situation, as we have said in an earlier chapter, can rob you of your motivation—or your mental and physical health. If Bob's well-being and sanity demand a more benign environment than Phil is likely to ever provide, then Bob has no choice. He must bail out and get another position.

But if Bob can tough this one out—without damaging his mind, body, or motivation—sticking with the game and seeing it for the game it is might be his best career move. He can even capitalize on Phil's absentee management style. Because Phil is rarely around and Bob is shouldering so much of the responsibility, the higher-ups in his own firm and the clients must know that he is a key player. If he shines in this position, without the shadow of Phil over him, his light will shine brightly.

If Your Boss Is Protecting His Rear

Perhaps your boss disappears because he is 100 percent focused on his own future. When the work is chancy and success unsure, some crafty bosses keep away until the outcomes are predictable. Then they swoop in at the last minute, either to take the credit or to shift all the blame onto you.

Sometimes the phantom boss is just a lazy fraud. If no one is looking over the boss's shoulder—say if she is the bank branch manager or the local store manager and there is no one above her at your location—she might be able to collect a salary without working to earn it. Dumping all the responsibility on you can give your evasive boss the freedom to spend hours in the gym or the trout stream. There is no end to the relaxed personal life an absentee boss can enjoy.

If your boss is just goofing off, you have a couple of choices, and which one you choose depends on what your absentee boss's position is in the company.

If Your Boss Owns the Business

If your boss owns the business, he may think he has a right to leave you alone all day and just show up to pick up the day's receipts. This is not the true entrepreneurial spirit, but it is the way some business owners think. In this situation, you may feel like a slave instead of an employee, especially if you are not well paid. Before you quit your job, lobby your boss to pay you enough to keep you there. State your case convincingly and you may be able to persuade him that you are essential. After all, you are, aren't you?

Consider this: If you can run the business for your boss, do you think you could run a competitive business all on your own? What would it take to set it up? How you might go about that is the subject of another book, but hey, it's worth asking yourself the questions and maybe writing a business plan.

If Your Boss Is Negligent

If you work for an absentee boss who doesn't own the business, but is getting away with not doing his job, you have a difficult and potentially dangerous question to ask yourself: Should you rat on him to the big boss? People who think of doing this are often looking to satisfy their well-developed sense of justice. They cannot stand seeing someone get away with this kind of fraudulent behavior. They also feel personally robbed: They are collecting an underling's salary and the boss gets the fat paycheck while they do all the work. This is bound to raise a person's fairness hackles.

Proceed with Caution

Before you snitch to the big boss, however, there are a few pitfalls that might make your quest for justice more trouble than it's worth.

Suppose the knavish boss is—unbeknownst to you—the big boss's sister's boyfriend. Maybe the big boss thinks the swindler will treat his sister right if he gives him a job. What good would it do you to try to right this wrong?

And that is the salient question here. What are you trying to accomplish by squealing? If you have a real goal in mind, then let's examine what it might be. We need to do a risk-benefit analysis.

If you are trying to right a wrong against your employer, and it is one you are reasonably sure your employer wants righted, then you may be able to do it, provided you do it in the right way. More about that in a moment. But understand that this is almost never a good idea.

If your only goal is do harm to your negligent boss, you might need to weigh that more carefully. You may be taking a pretty big risk for little benefit to yourself—especially if all you are going to get out of it is some minor league gloating.

The Flip Side

On the other hand, Machiavelli might have something to say about this. It may be that pointing out to the big boss that your boss is not doing her job will get you a crack at a promotion. I am not suggesting finking as a way to get ahead, although knowing how many mendacious two-timers there are in this world, I would imagine that I just put a rotten idea in some people's minds. In assessing the risk of spilling the beans on your boss, you need to put on the plus side that you may be in line for his job if he gets fired for not doing it. That outcome might not be unjust.

On the risk side of your balance sheet, you need to put the possibility that, when not at his desk, your boss is doing favors for the big boss. In that case, you could lose your job instead.

Look for Advantages

In end, you have to admit that as frustrating as an absentee boss is, working for a person who is not around that much has its advantages. Remember Erich Nilsson, the guy at the beginning of this chapter, who had to present at an important meeting with almost no information to go on. Well, here's the truth about him—the real person whose story this is: The people at the meeting constituted the top management of his company. Erich aced that presentation, and the executives were so impressed, they invited him to speak again, this time at the parent company's annual meeting. Within six weeks of giving that stab-in-the-dark presentation, he got a promotion.

Sometimes what comes up from the watery depths is a monster; sometimes it carries a golden apple of opportunity in its mouth.

When to Surrender

The greatest danger of operating in the realm of the Loch Ness Monster is that the beast can suddenly come up from the bottom of the lake and upset your boat. Evasive creatures, especially if they are humans, can be purposely elusive because they are cagey or deceitful. If this is true for you, review the strategies in the preceding chapter on a deceitful boss behaving like an Abominable Snowman and weigh whether it's worth it to take action.

Some people thrive in this type of pressure cooker. If you are reading this book, looking for ways to cope with a particularly elusive boss, you obviously want to find a way to survive. Sometimes all this means is toughing it out. If you can do that without being overcome by the toxic fumes your boss exudes, you can triumph in the end. If you think it's not worth it, stop wasting your time. Get away from the poison as soon as you can.

10

DRACULA
THE BLOODSUCKER WHO DRAINS YOU DRY

Renfield: "No, Master. No. Please, please do not ask me to do that."
Count Dracula: "Obey."
Script of the 1931 movie, *Dracula*

"There are a lot of potential clients to evaluate on that list, George. I must have a file on each one, including a download of their Web sites by ten a.m. tomorrow. Stop wasting my time and get to it."

Upper management admired George's boss, Frankie. She ran a tight ship. They liked her no nonsense management style. No sense at all is how George thought of it.

By eleven that evening, bleary eyed from staring at the computer screen for nearly ten hours, feeling a bit delirious from fatigue and lack of real food, George began to fantasize about why Frankie had expected such a gargantuan task to be completed in such an obviously inadequate amount of time. She is testing me, he thought, stretching his aching neck and covering his burning eyes. She wants to see if I will crack under the pressure.

At 2 A.M., crunching on spearmint lifesavers, the only form of sustenance left in his office, George started nodding off with his hands on the keyboard. When the night guard came by at 2:30 A.M., he tapped George's shoulder. "Why don't you go home and get some shuteye?" George accepted the guard's offer to walk him to his car and chat to help him wake up enough to drive the fifteen miles home.

The next morning Frankie rolled her eyes when George came in—on time, but not early. "Well?" she greeted him.

He admitted that he was only 80 percent done.

"This is not school," she growled. "Eighty percent is not a passing grade. Either the job is done on time, or you are a complete failure."

George did not respond.

Frankie blew out her breath and did her special eye roll again. "You have an hour and a half. Get it done."

Completely deflated, George gave Frankie what he thought she deserved. He skipped a lot of pages in the downloads of the Web sites and, worse yet, in a couple of instances, he filled in the potential client's net revenue on the spreadsheet with numbers he guessed at instead of actually looking them up on Dun & Bradstreet reports.

When Frankie came by at 9:45 A.M. to pick up the reports, she glanced over them and gave him a skeptical look. She knows, he thought. Now she'll fire me for fudging the report. He actually tried to feel guilty, but he really couldn't feel anything through the caffeine jitters.

George had started that job full of hope and energy. Now, after two years of working for Vampire Woman, he felt defeated and compelled to cheat, which left him frightened and filled with self-doubt.

Identifying Dracula Behavior

Would you be surprised to know that Bram Stoker—the creator of Dracula—had a legendarily horrible boss? Sir Henry Irving, an English actor and impresario was known as a boss from hell, a man who fed off the energies of others. Stoker, subjected to Irving's fits of ego and temper, wrote the story of an undead monster that begins on Walpurgisnacht and ends with a stake through the heart of the bloodsucker.

You don't need to check for your manager's image in a mirror or catch her sleeping in a coffin to figure out if she's a Dracula. You probably imagine she carries a whip under her cape that she happily wields to extract the maximum amount of work from her people, often without regard to whether it is even possible to produce the desired result at all, much less to produce it at a satisfactory level. Bloodsucking bosses and organizations say they want to "challenge" the employee to produce as much as possible. The fangs they use are many.

Dracula bosses believe in the law of supply and demand: you supply; they demand. They overwork you and begrudge you your rewards. These autocrats believe that the only way to succeed is at someone else's expense. Some oppressive overachievers set unrealistic standards for themselves as well as for other people. The superambitious may expect her staff to share her neurotic workaholism.

Everybody is capable of peak productivity, extra-strength work levels in a crunch. When an emergency brings on an adrenalin high, off we go speeding to the finish line. But this kind of performance is only okay in real emergencies for finite periods of time. Company organization and work structures that require this most of the time become abusive and, in the long run, counterproductive, both for the organization and for the employee. If a Dracula boss drains you completely, you can only give bloodless performance. And do not for a moment forget that vampires are made when their victims are bitten too often. If you stay in such a job long enough and succeed at it, you could become a vampire too.

In some cases people are not paid for their extra work. Or their pay is kept as low as possible. Their managements see their employees' salaries not as an investment in their human capital, but as a cost to be reduced to the lowest possible levels, if not eliminated. Our economy is troubled right now. But even when it is growing, wages frequently don't keep pace. In 2004, the American economy expanded for the third straight year. Yet that same year, the Census Bureau reported that the average household income had not increased in five years. In fact, in real terms, it had fallen. Vampires take blood; they do not give it.

When the economy is in eclipse, Dracula bosses get worse. Their normal behavior might be to threaten people with being fired if they do not perform. In a downturn, those threats have sharper teeth because another job will be harder to find. Bloodsuckers may seduce employees with promises of raises and promotions that do not materialize. Getting the promised reward will be even less likely if the company's bottom line is already suffering. Chintzy bosses give people too much work and do not give them the proper tools, supplies, and technology. Again bad times make these conditions more likely.

Corporate Reality

Organizations cut staff way back and then expect the remaining skeleton crew to do at least as much as, if not more than, the larger staff used to do. No wonder they call that a skeleton crew and refer to this organization style as "lean and mean."

There is nothing wrong with a company trying to keep itself profitable by eliminating excess staff—sometimes management absolutely must eliminate jobs to save the organization. One of the worst things a company can do to its employees is go out of business—and they all lose their jobs. Yet many organizations make extreme cutbacks to increase profitability. In the process, they leave their people with no hope of keeping up with the workload. The pressure for quantity of work prevents employees from producing high-quality work. Overtaxed workers often sink into a bog of lost motivation, frustration, stress, and pure exhaustion. No one can do top-notch work under these circumstances. Who wants to spend her entire work life producing lackluster results under battle conditions? Besides, the resulting levels of fatigue and frustration can and do lead to ill health—and destroy mental health—including substance abuse and abuse within the family. What kind of price is that to pay? Who are the monstrous or the clueless who would exact such a toll in the name of productivity? Dracula bosses can and do.

The Techno Squeeze

Modern work life keeps more and more people on call twenty-four/seven. You may have been happy when your boss gave you that cell phone, that BlackBerry, and a high-speed Internet connection at home. Wow, you thought, I am on the cutting edge. Except that now you know that that cutting edge is on your boss's secondary incisors and that he is sinking them into your neck. Those seemingly sexy high-tech gadgets mean that you never know when an e-mail is going to bling into your pocket during your kid's basketball game or a cell phone call from a customer is going to squeal you away from a dinner with your dad. If you are working all hours, remember, vampires do their dastardly deeds in the night.

Work More, Receive Less

Another potential performance pressure cooker arrives disguised as a great opportunity—the promise of high-performance pay, where people who produce more get paid more. Done properly, this can be a very positive way for companies to reward their best people, who merit bonuses because they contribute more to the bottom line. People in such jobs report higher levels of job satisfaction. They enjoy more self-respect when they have to stretch and do more than coast along at work. They feel accomplished, they learn, they get a greater sense of their own potency as human beings. This is all to the good, especially if it comes with a bigger paycheck—unless it gets out of hand.

If the top levels of pay are quite high and are linked to superhuman levels of performance, people can get on a treadmill they cannot get off. They produce like crazy to qualify for the higher pay, they make more money, and then they need more money to support a higher life style. Before they know it, they cannot get a breather. Result: their attempt to maintain super-high levels of performance over too long a period of time leads to super-high levels of stress, which can bring about heart disease, high blood pressure, and, again, drug and alcohol abuse.

Working all the time can kill you. Years ago, on a business trip to Japan, I learned that the Japanese actually have a word for it: *karoshi*. It means death from overwork. At the time, there was a case being reported there in the press. A garage attendant at a big company had a regular work schedule of twelve hours on and twelve hours off. Disaster struck when his coworker who was to relieve him did not show up for work. He stayed on and worked the other guy's shift. Then, of course it was his turn again. After thirty-six consecutive hours of work, he went home and died. In those days, *karoshi* was such a common occurrence in Japan that you could actually buy a specific insurance policy against it. The public became outraged when the insurance company refused a death benefit to the garage attendant's poor family because he died after he got home, and not on the job.

Well, you may say, yes in Japan, years back, but not here, not now. But this we do know: In one study, 25 percent of people reported that they experienced excessive pressure to perform. And the average American works 350 more hours per year than the average German. That's like working ten more weeks a year!

Twenty years ago, Americans boasted about being workaholics. Hopefully we can learn to grow into more fully developed people, rather than making ourselves slaves to the job, unable to savor life's pleasures. People very like us in other countries have productive economies without acting as if they live in anthills. Why not us?

Strategies for Coping with Dracula Behavior

If you are being overworked at these levels, how can you protect yourself from being completely drained by the Count Dracula in the corner office? Strew your cubicle with wolf bane? Wear a wreath of garlic around your neck? If only those tactics would work. Unfortunately, there are no magic potions. You have to find the courage to do something *before* you have a heart attack or a stroke.

Discuss the Problem

Start by talking to your boss about the levels of demand. See if you cannot convince him that the quality of your work will be better if you work at a quick, but deliberate pace. Point out the errors and lost opportunities that are the result of having too few resources brought to bear in reaching the organization's goals.

Make Your Efforts Obvious

With a slave driver, if you work with grace and never break a sweat, you may convince the boss that you are not putting in any effort. I am not suggesting that you "look busy" to avoid a legitimate amount of work. But if you are being overworked, you may have to show the effort you are putting in. Keep the piles of work on your desk—not out of sight. Walk fast when you go the printer to pick up your work. Keep your fingers on the keyboard, even when you are thinking of what to type next.

Get Off the Bonus Pay Treadmill

You may take home less money, but at least you will keep your sanity and improve your family life. Your boss may give lip service to being a decent employer, and you may see that as hypocritical. But then you have to think about the lip service you give to putting your family first.

In fact, recent studies show that more people report that they are happier with their jobs than they are satisfied with their family lives. There may be many reasons why this would be true. Most likely, we ask more of our family lives than we do of our jobs. But think about this. If for whatever reason you enjoy your job more than your life away from work, you may actually want to spend all those long hours on the job.

Examine Your Role

If you cannot bring yourself to fight back against unreasonable demands, you may be conflicted about the need to work so hard. You may resent being overworked and underappreciated, but you may also use work as an escape. You have to decide this for yourself. If you are throwing yourself into your work to escape problems elsewhere, you are not the first person on this planet to do so. But at least relieve yourself of the stress of feeling put upon by your workload. Admit to yourself that you want to work really hard. Then you can do your demanding job with enthusiasm and pleasure, and make all that work therapeutic instead of super stressful. If you let yourself believe that your heavy workload is a terrible burden instead of something that deep down you actually welcome, then the pressure of having to perform it will only add to the pressures you feel in your personal life. Doubling your trouble is not a solution to anything.

(You must realize, however, that escaping your personal problems by drowning your sorrows in work probably means that you are neglecting your family, disregarding your personal growth, and ignoring the needs of your community.

Avoidance of these life issues will not make them go away. The fatigue of overwork may help you forget them, but when you wake up, they will still be there. As people in AA will tell you, oblivion does not mean the trouble disappears. Denial is not just a river in Egypt.)

Ask for a Raise

It is surprising how many people are afraid to ask for a raise. Yet, if you work for a bloodsucker, your only chance at a salary increase may be to out-and-out ask for one. This takes courage, but you can do it without being overly aggressive or brassy. Here are some techniques that will help you.

Do a Comparative Analysis

Plan your campaign. Your greatest asset here will be to know your organization's salary practices. In most decent-size organizations, this information should be readily available from HR. Perhaps the rules are published in the company's policy and procedures manual.

Find out what people who do what you do make in competitive organizations. You can usually get this information by looking at job postings in your category. If your work is unusual and there aren't many jobs like yours, this could be to your advantage—people with special skills are usually paid more. On the other hand, if there aren't very many jobs in your category in your area, you may not have many choices about where to work. That will limit your ability to pressure your boss for more money.

Set Your Target Amount

Decide on a specific amount of money that you think you should get. The information above should point to a reasonable figure that is within the corporate guidelines and puts you in line with what others who do similar work are getting.

Prepare a rationale for why you deserve this raise. Base your appeal on business judgment, not your financial situation. Companies do not pay people based on their needs; they set salaries based on their employees' contribution and what the labor market will bear. Use the data you have collected on what is generally paid for similar work in your area or your company. Print out ads from Web sites or cut ads out of trade journals or the newspaper.

Document Your Successes

Document your contribution to your work group. Be ready to give your boss a brief rundown of successful projects you have done since your last raise. If your job has become more demanding, have some data handy on just how and when it changed. If you have taken the initiative to make yourself or your group more efficient, remind the boss of what you did. Bring in copies of e-mails or notes you have received from other people, especially from customers or people in other departments that your group serves.

Plan a matter-of-fact presentation. It may make you uncomfortable to have to remind the boss of how good you are at your job, but it will be worth it.

Choose an Opportune Time

Timing is important. Approach the boss before your regular salary review is due. If you wait until afterward, there may be nothing he can do to change a raise that has just been approved. If you get there ahead of time, at least your boss will know what you expect, and she may be able to influence your raise amount for the better.

When you request an appointment, tell the boss that you want to discuss your salary. Unless he is a super skinflint, it will be better for you if he knows what you want to talk about. (If he is tight-fisted when it comes to money, say you want to talk about your work *and* your contribution. This will be technically true.) Set up the meeting for a conference room. This will make it more comfortable for you than doing it in your boss's office.

As you enter the meeting, picture yourself coming out with a big smile on your face, proud of how you conducted yourself, and happy about how the boss responded. Keep any negative images of the boss's reaction out of your mind or you might inadvertently make them come true.

Stay Focused

At the meeting, keep a professional demeanor. Stay calm but be assertive. Try to imagine that you are discussing the department's budget, not something personal. Present your request and your rationale. Mention that you want to maintain your motivation. It is fair to say, "A raise right now will help me maintain my high level of dedication to my job. It will show me that you and the company appreciate my contribution."

Use supportive communication techniques. Be brief. Be clear.

Stay on Message

If you get turned down, ask why. Say: "It will help me accept your decision if I know exactly why you are saying no."

No matter the reason, ask for advice. If she says, "Now is not the time," be gracious and ask when will be the right time. Then when you come back at the appointed time, you will have the advantage. In fact at that point, you will begin by saying, "Four months ago when I came to ask you for a raise, you suggested that this month would be the best time for us to talk about it." This will make it sound as if you are only following orders.

If your boss tells you that she does not have authority to grant you a raise, ask her permission to talk to the person who does. Also ask her if she agrees that you deserve a raise. Say you would like to tell the person in authority that your boss supports you in this.

If he turns you down because he thinks you do not deserve a raise, ask what you have to do make yourself eligible. Then you can weigh his demands. If you can and you want to, you can meet them to strengthen your case for the next time.

If the company is in a slump that precludes anyone getting a raise, ask for other kinds of compensation—extra time off, permission to attend training programs.

End on a congenial note. Never make threats to try to extort a raise. If you think you have to threaten to leave to get a raise, and you are willing to do that, why not just leave? Whatever you decide to do, ultimately, you are going to have to work with this boss a little longer. Make it as pleasant as possible.

When to Surrender

If you have tried everything, it's time to stop feeling like a dupe. Short of driving a stake through his black heart, you may find the only way to fend off your boss's blood-sucking tendencies is to make an exit plan and leave. In the meantime, do a reasonable amount of work. If you get threatened with dismissal, beat him to the punch—implement your exit strategy before you join the ranks of the undead. Find ways to cope in your last weeks on this job. Use passive resistance to avoid complete slavery. Be placid, work hard, but do only what is reasonable. Clam up while your boss is on the rampage. While you are looking for a better job, understand that you are staying *temporarily* because you need a paycheck until you find your next position. If you remind yourself that you are there by choice, you will reduce your stress and stop feeling like a dupe.

11

DR. JEKYLL AND MR. HYDE

SUBSTANCE ABUSE AND
OTHER MENTAL INSTABILITIES

"I've done nothing. I am Dr. Henry Jekyll. I have done nothing."
Dr. Jekyll in the 1941 movie script for *Dr. Jekyll and Mr. Hyde*

Annamaria Mantegna negotiated contracts with suppliers for her office equipment manufacturing company. The firm was about to come to market with a new printer/copier/scanner. Getting the new product launched quickly was critical, but pricing was also important. Annamaria focused all her energy analyzing the merits of time versus price. In the end, she was convinced that grabbing market share early was more important than pricing. "I think this product will outshine the competition, but only if we can beat them to market with this new technology. We have to go for early timing and not worry if our product winds up costing $100 more than the competition."

TJ, her boss, nodded gravely. "Are you sure?"

Annamaria was sure. Her next step was to prepare for negotiations with the supplier of components for the new product. She focused on timing and presented TJ her data, the market research reports, the sales projections, the competitive pricing analysis. She went over with TJ the alternatives for what course of action to employ with a supplier of the casing units. Finally, TJ agreed on a strategy—they would pay a bit more for each unit, but they would take delivery in six months.

On her way to the negotiation meeting, Annamaria beamed with enthusiasm. She had everything in place. When the suppliers came into the conference room, she took her place next to TJ. Just as she was about to distribute her agenda, along with her charts and graphs of the delivery schedule, TJ smiled and said, "Let me just say to begin with that our most important objective here is price. We can be flexible about your delivery schedule, but we have to keep the cost down."

Annamaria had to clench her jaw not to let it drop. TJ had flipped 180 degrees away from their planned course of action. It wasn't the first time he had done something like this, but it shocked Annamaria nonetheless. She turned her neat stack of paperwork face down on the conference room table like a poker player folding a hand.

What would cause TJ to do such an about-face? Had he gotten information from someone else that canceled Annamaria's arguments? Did he receive word from his own boss that upper management thought price was more important? If so, why hadn't he clued her in before this meeting? Who or what was pulling his strings to make him completely change course?

Identifying Jekyll and Hyde Behavior

Does your boss criticize you one minute, praise you the next? Is he a liar, or does he just have a short attention span? Does he have multiple-personality disorder?

Some bosses change all the time for the sake of change or because they believe the last person they talked to. They constantly switch priorities or rethink decisions. These flip-floppers keep people off guard, force them to guess what is really needed and how to please them—a management style that causes not only stress, but also tons of wasted effort. Deadlines loom and the team is running about in eight different directions trying to get clarity on the actual goal of the work.

Some bosses—like TJ—blow in the wind. They change directions for reasons known only to them. But we can imagine what might be ailing them. Vacillators are often uncomfortable with power. They try to do their jobs, but they haven't got the guts to stick to their guns. They make a decision, but they become so fearful that it might backfire that they unmake it and make a different one. They spend so much time trying to see all sides of the issue—to make sure they haven't missed anything important—that they never make up their mind. This analysis paralysis transmits indecision or less urgency than the situation merits.

Other bosses change things just for the sake of change. Something new comes along and they always want to try it. This can be good and even fun, but fixing things that are not broken eats up the budget. Unnecessary spending may mean you will not get a bonus at the end of the year.

Some bosses are consistently inconsistent—like the ones who play favorites—Dr. Jekyll giving every perk to his chosen few; Mr. Hyde giving all the drudge work to those who are not in his little clique.

False promisers and Indian givers also fall into this category. Danglers promise raises and promotions, contingent upon your complying with some wish of theirs or some extra effort on your part. You do what they require, but then when the time comes for the boss to deliver, she doesn't. Sometimes whole organizations can promise one thing, but deliver another. Take Raul Woodson's boss, Mike, for instance. He went around quoting Dr. Peter Drucker—the great management thinker. "As Drucker said" was the way he always started when he was about to wax philosophical about management. "Business's most important asset is its people" was his favorite Drucker quote. If Raul heard Mike say that once, he heard it a hundred times. The first time was when Raul interviewed for his job with the bond rating firm where Mike became his boss.

At first, Raul was thrilled to get a job with a company that promised its employees flexibility. Mike spoke with complete conviction about the company's commitment to its employees. "We need to attract and keep the best people. This company requires the greatest level of skills and loyalty from its people. To attract and keep them, we need to give them greater control over their lives. We're not a huge, impersonal company. All of us here are family oriented. We can be generous with time off for family matters. It's all here in the Human Resources Policy and Procedures Manual."

And the manual agreed, in black and white. Buck, Cantowitz & Cole offered Raul just what he wanted. Married four years and ready to start a family, he and his wife, Alice, wanted his next job to be one where he could take time off when the baby came, that gave him regular hours so that he could get home at a reasonable time to be with his family, the ability—once Alice went back to lawyering—to be flexible if the baby got sick. Buck, Cantowitz's stated policies suited Raul perfectly. The actual practices, not at all.

Reality struck soon after Raul took the job. His coworkers worked long hours—totally gung-ho, totally committed—even the ones who had kids, even when their kids were sick. They talked to their babysitters on the phone, instructed them to take the baby to the doctor, talked to the doctor on the phone, but they did not rush off the way the Policy Manual said they could. What they were allowed to do under the rules and what they actually did differed completely. When Raul's wife gave birth a year and a half later, Raul had already seen the handwriting on the wall: It said, "Do what we do, not what we say, or forget about a great career here."

Mike, Raul's boss, said all the right things, but it was lip service. Those benign Dr. Jekyll communications had nothing to do with the Mr. Hyde reality. Raul had to decide—his career at Buck, Cantowitz or his family. Raul decided to go against the company's prevailing culture. He chose to take advantage of the stated policy. If little Joshua needed him, he stayed home. He and Alice took turns. He left work at 6 most evenings—so he could be home to give his baby a bath and rock or read him to sleep. He did his job very well, but he did not do it for twelve hours a day. His career stalled. But he stuck to his family-oriented guns.

If you work for a bait-and-switch company, these are your choices. Knuckle under and do what everyone else does or buck the trend, take them at their word, and do what they say you have a right to do. Or you can go elsewhere. But be careful. The next time an organization states a policy, ask the right questions during the interview process. See if you can talk to people who will be your coworkers. Find out if what you hear is what you will see.

Some vacillators are highly neurotic; some are so seriously bent that they need medical attention. But remember, since you are not qualified to treat the sick, what you need to develop is a way of dealing with these bosses, not how to cure them.

Strategies for Coping with Jekyll and Hyde Behavior

How you deal with your changeable boss will depend on why she can't make a decision and stick to it. Is it insecurity, indecisiveness, uncertainty? Does he play favorites? Or is he a drunk or a drug abuser who changes when he is high?

If Your Boss Vacillates

If your boss tells everyone a different story, could it be that he is hiding something and purposely spreading confusion instead of the truth? Does she use her different interpretations to placate employees with different points of view? To squelch everyone's opinions? Does she pretend to agree with everyone just to keep "peace in the family?"

If your boss is this changeable, you need to take some steps to give yourself a degree of consistency. If you cannot trust your boss to follow through on promises or stick to her decisions, confirm them in writing. For instance, if she changes priorities and assignments often and capriciously, you can shoot her an e-mail that says, "Dear Fran, Just to recap our meeting today about priorities—I am going to concentrate on the cost-effectiveness project. You will ask Howard to take over the new packaging financial analysis. Let me know if I haven't got this right." It is likely that your boss will see through this attempt to get her to stick to her agreements. That could be good. Maybe bringing the issue a bit more out in the open will cause her to think twice before pulling her usual switcheroo.

If Your Boss Plays Favorites

If your boss plays favorites and you are not one of the chosen, I am sorry to say that there is probably not much you can do to make him evenhanded. I know, it is like being back in high school, where you were either in the in-crowd or you weren't. But some people become bosses without ever growing up. Make an attempt to right the situation by calling him on it. Say: "Jonathan, Mary, and Richard have gotten to go to the last couple of annual meetings. I would love an opportunity to go, too." I had a boss once who was astonished that I would want to go out of town overnight on business since I had a child at home. A widower who had never had children, he always picked people without families to do the traveling because he thought the other employees would not want to be away from their kids. All I had to do to change his mind was ask for what I wanted.

If Your Boss Is Insecure

Muriel Solomon worked in an insurance company as a cost analyst. She was good at her job and got along well with the other people in her group. She was, frankly, surprised when they made her manager of her team. One of her main worries was that the people who used to be her friends would no longer like her. So when she first took over as manager, she tried very hard to stay low key, not to come across as bossy. She respected the other analysts' ability to do their jobs. She hoped that would be enough. She left them pretty much on their own.

Soon she noticed a drop in productivity. She concluded that they were goofing off and decided to watch for signs of time wasting and to nip them in the bud. When she saw people talking together, she scolded them for socializing instead of working. Soon the whole place was buzzing with the news that Muriel had turned into a tyrant, that her promotion had gone to her head.

Next Muriel noticed that people were avoiding her, looking very busy when she came by. Then she decided that she must have overdone the whip cracking. She did not want them to think of her as a shrew. So she tried to make her people understand that she still wanted to be friends with them. She went around chatting everyone up, asking them about their families and how their weekend was, what vacation plans did they have. Then when she saw them chatting with one another, she decided they were taking advantage of her friendly attitude. She turned cold and scolding again.

If your Dr. Jekyll and Mr. Hyde's vacillation stems from fear, there are some straightforward ways to deal with it. First, recognize and deal with your own self-doubts. If you don't know what you are afraid of, what you avoid confronting and why, you will never know if it is the boss's fears or you own that are causing the problem.

Learn to boost the boss's confidence in you and your work. Research and back up your recommendations with data and a strong rationale. Reassure the boss so he will have the courage to stand by your advice.

Write up decisions. When you and the boss agree on something, put your conclusions in an e-mail. Putting things in writing may seem like an old-fashioned bureaucratic habit, but at least you will have a record if things go awry. Also, a minor league vacillator may be deterred from changing his mind if he has an e-mail in his inbox documenting his decision. You never know.

If Your Boss Has an Addiction

It strikes me as no coincidence that Robert Louis Stevenson turned Dr. Jekyll into Mr. Hyde by having him drink a potion. Drugs and alcohol are the cause of a lot of "mood swings," especially in high-stakes jobs—like finance, law, or surgery. Twenty-two million people in the United States have serious drug or alcohol problems. A fair number of them are managers and supervisors. Armies of people work for bosses who can function only before lunch. Once they go out and have a few drinks or a snort of cocaine in lieu of a tuna sandwich, they are not worth much in the afternoon. These substance abusers sometimes also become employee abusers.

Lindsey Gordon had a thorny situation. Bryce, her boss, was moody—always overly friendly in the morning, completely cold the afternoon. "If he were a woman my mother's age" she told her friend Barbara, "I would say he was menopausal." They laughed.

A few weeks later, they had nothing to laugh at. Lindsey went to Bryce's office to ask him a question. Bryce was running out the door when she arrived, and his phone was ringing. "Get that please," he asked quickly. "I'm late for a client lunch. If it's them, tell them I'll be there in four minutes." He sped to the elevator, and Lindsey jogged over to his phone. It wasn't the client on the line. It was Bryce's sister, who needed Bryce to get back to her and needed to give Lindsey a callback number.

Lindsey scanned Bryce's desk for a scrap of paper, and not seeing one handy, she absently mindedly opened his top left-hand drawer. What she saw in there stopped her mind cold.

"Hello. Hello," his sister said. "Can you hear me?"

"Yes. Yes," Lindsey blurted out. "I'm—I'm trying to find a scrap of paper to write on."

"I know how his desk his," his sister said.

But what Lindsey saw in the drawer was beyond messy. She picked up a ballpoint and wrote the number on her hand. The shadow of it was still there when she met Barbara for a drink after work.

"Drug paraphernalia?" Barbara said.

"Yeah. Just like you see on *Law and Order.* That rubber thingy that they tie around their arm. A needle. A dirty spoon, whatever that's for."

"Good God!"

"What do I do?"

What, indeed? If the boss is an addict, what does an employee do to stop him from self- and organizational destruction? This is a very tricky problem.

Be Observant

First, short of finding drug paraphernalia in her desk drawer, how can you tell if your boss has this problem? First of all, keep in mind that substance abuse could be what's causing your boss's bad behaviors. Lot's of employees might dismiss this idea, but considering the odds, it might be true of your Mr. Hyde. Don't think it can't be. It can.

Watch out for sudden shifts in behavior, especially if they occur regularly after a paycheck, after lunch, after he disappears for a while. Do his hands shake? Does that shaking go away after he goes out and comes back?

Avoid Rescue Fantasies

If you suspect substance abuse and you really like your boss and your job, you may have rescue fantasies—imagining that you can intervene and save him from himself. Put this notion out of your mind. Confronting alcoholics or addicts and telling them what they are doing is wrong doesn't reform them. Robert Louis Stevenson must have known this. Look back at the quote at the beginning of this chapter. Substance abusers are very likely to deny there is a problem. They already know what they are doing is not right. Their addiction is a botched attempt to deal with what they cannot otherwise deal with in their own lives. Most of them cannot pay the price of giving it up. Besides, there is a very low success rate with alcohol or drug abuse treatment, even when addicts are treated by professionals. Given that you are not a professional in this field, you should not even begin to try to fix the boss's problem.

Assess the Situation

Okay, so you are not going to be able to save your boss. What can you do? First you have to assess the situation. Ask yourself some questions:

- How does this person's behavior affect my personal success?
- Can he sink my reputation with his erratic behavior?
- If this is a fixed and intractable problem, how is it likely to affect the long-term success of our team? Our division? The company as a whole?
- Where is this person in the chain of command?

- Is drug or alcohol abuse common among people at her level in the company?
- What is likely to be the attitude of those in the chain of command that I might talk to about this?
- What is the corporate culture? Is there a stated policy? Is it enforced, or likely to be?

You need to determine how dangerous it would be to talk to someone about what you suspect. Be forewarned that doing anything can blow up in your face. If you try to talk to your addicted boss about his problem, he may go bonkers on you—not only deny it, which would be pretty normal, but accuse you of lying, of being insubordinate, of trying to steal his job. He may get furious, shout that you are scheming against him. He might fire you on the spot.

You can expect a stronger reaction if the problem is drugs, rather than alcohol. Drugs are illegal. Alcohol, no matter how much of it people ingest and no matter how impaired it makes them, is legal. Not that telling him you think he is a drunk is going to endear you to him, but at least, you wouldn't be calling him a felon.

On the other hand, anyone else you talk to in the firm might brush off your concerns about alcohol by saying that your boss is just a social drinker.

Caution: Don't Put It in Writing

In either case, you may go to your boss's boss or to HR with the problem, but let me be ABSOLUTELY clear on this: TALK about the problem. Do not write about it. Even if the person you are reporting it to asks you to write about it. Say that you feel uncomfortable putting your suspicions into writing. Remind whoever it is that you are not the person in the firm in charge of enforcing substance-abuse rules and that you are just trying to help make things better by revealing the situation.

Be Fully Prepared

Remember the exit plan that I suggested in Chapter 3? Do not—under any circumstances—discuss your boss's substance abuse problems without having your exit plan completely thought out. There is an excellent chance that you will need it in this extremely touchy situation.

When to Back Off

You may want to let the whole thing slide. If your own work life is not all that affected and you can work around the boss's vagaries, you may want to do so. If you think you are not going to get anywhere by talking to him or anyone else, and you cannot operate with the difficulties his addiction creates, then you may want to just slip away to another job. Do not feel like a traitor. You did not create this problem. It is not yours to fix.

If He Has Dementia

Before we leave this subject of changeable bosses, there is one other possible cause of inconsistent behavior that is also quite touchy, but may have nothing to do with substances, legal or illegal. Suppose you have a boss who is getting on in years who doesn't stick with what he said because he cannot remember what he said. This is a potentially tragic situation.

Depending on how bad it is, you can write him notes to help him remember—at least to document what he said to you. You can try to protect him by compensating for his losses. On the other hand, if this boss is difficult because he is demented, it will do no one any good if you help him hide that from the organization. Ultimately, depending on the strength of your relationship with him, you may be able to talk to him about what you see. Would it be a betrayal to point out the problem to Human Resources?

If you are reading this book, you are already deeply troubled by your boss's dysfunctional behavior; you may think of her as a monster. The milk of human kindness might ordinarily encourage us to take pity on an aging person with a potentially awful problem, but if dementia has made him mean, you may not feel like helping him. Whatever you feel, you may need to do something for the good of the organization. If he owns the business, talk to his family. Otherwise, go to HR with the issue. There are ways for families and organizations to handle this problem, and handling them sooner is usually a whole lot better than handling them later—after the impaired person has been left to make destructive decisions.

When to Surrender

How serious are the underlying problems causing your boss's flip-flop behavior? How have you fared in your attempts to rectify the situation? If you have an intractable vacillator or a confirmed alcoholic as a boss, you might as well go and ply your trade somewhere else. With such a captain, your ship is going to founder sooner or later. Move along.

12

THE MUMMY

THE BOSS WHO DOESN'T COMMUNICATE

"Good heavens, what a terrible curse."
Script for the 1932 movie *The Mummy*

Joe Giacosa loved his job. He worked for the director of development, helping to raise money for an arts organization. It thrilled Joe when children from poor neighborhoods got to hear live music or see professional dance performances because of his behind-the-scenes efforts. Joe wanted to become great at what he did, but Jason, his boss, gave him only vague answers to his questions about the whys and wherefores of their work. Joe never got a bead on the big picture.

Whenever Joe asked his boss to talk about the strategy behind decisions, Jason shared nothing substantive. The more Joe tried to get in on things, the more resistant Jason became, until Joe found himself doing projects with no clear direction. Jason seemed to be expecting Joe to figure things out for himself. He seemed happy when Joe tried things that failed. Joe complained to his sister Nancy. "He makes me shoot first, and then he holds up the target and shows me that I missed."

Identifying Mummy Behavior

I did not choose the title of this chapter because some resurrected ancient Egyptian is a metaphor for a managerial flaw. The Mummy boss is a pain because her credo is "Mum's the word."

We are dealing with the supervisor who never lets you know where you stand, never compliments you on your work—not to you and not to anyone else who might be in a position to help further your career. He never explains his decisions.

This chapter will also cover the opposite problem: the boss who blabs your secrets or uses personal information against you. But let's start with the tight-lipped, the taciturn, the reticent.

Monster Mummy bosses are not just those who don't talk much, don't thank you for a job well-done, or don't even say good morning. There are managers who are shy or evasive, never look you in the eye. These can be difficult. We wish we could feel a little warmth from them, have a friendly chat once in a while, but mostly these people, while chilly, are not all that problematic. But there are specific kinds of reticence that can make life at work a horror show.

Mummies come wrapped in linen. I have an image of a different scary movie creature wrapped in white gauze, in an old black-and-white movie I saw on TV as a child: Claude Raines in *The Invisible Man*. He takes off the bandages and there is no one there. Bosses who do not lead you to success are leading you nowhere. Or, worse yet, off a career cliff.

Corporate Reality

In modern workplaces, managerial taciturnity may be a matter of corporate policy. If what you want from your boss is clarity about your future, you may be asking too much. He may legitimately fear that you will take any description he offers as a promise he may not be able to keep. Besides, organizations used to make clear career paths for their employees, but many organizations no longer do this. They view your future career as your own province and your own problem. Demanding information about what the organization is going to do for you may yield nothing because the organization makes no such promises.

Likewise, you may want more clarity than the company wants to give about policies and structures. As we said in Chapter 5, modern corporations have changed in this regard. If you used to work for a company that had well-defined rules, roles, and reasons why, you may think your latest employer should have the same. But corporate rigidity is not the wave of the future. Many companies have loose, fluid structures these days in the hopes that they can foster creativity by jettisoning the policy and procedures manual. It is a mistake for organizations to do this without clearly and carefully defining their goals and objectives. You should not expect some organizations to tell you exactly how you should go about your work, not these days. If your boss gives you leeway, let this flexibility release your creativity. On the other hand, if the company doesn't really make clear its own goals, then the whole company may soon become completely mummified.

Strategies for Coping with Mummy Behavior

If you have a boss who never tells you how your goals mesh with the organization's goals, never lets you in on things, or gives you only vague direction, this boss is stunting your growth. You cannot progress in your career if your manager refuses to teach you what you need to know.

Play on Your Boss's Team

Can you imagine what might motivate a boss to lead his people toward failure? Yup. Fear. If he is afraid that you will surpass him, take his job, he will make sure that you do not look good in the eyes of others in the organization. You can be pretty sure of this if one of the ways he keeps mum is never to introduce you to or give you a chance to "perform" in front of top-level people.

One way to try to deal with such jealousy is to approach your fearful boss in supportive terms. Though you have every right to expect support from your boss, rather than having to pussyfoot around his fears, you may have to turn the tables and reassure him. Like the movie hero who approaches the nasty cur with the words, "Nice doggy. Nice doggy." Try saying "we" rather than "I," as in "Maybe *we* can impress top management by solving this problem ourselves. What is *the organization's* objective here?" If this gets you the information you need, okay. If you can convince your boss that you are his ally in his quest for recognition and job security, you may be able to make him confident enough to confide in you. This can make your own work life more rewarding and interesting.

The caveat is, of course, that your boss may take your solutions to problems and sell them as his own. This is a pretty common ploy of bad managers. Some of them actually believe that they deserve the credit for everything invented by the people who work for them. That might be acceptable, but only if they also take the blame for all the mistakes of their employees. However, many try to have it both ways, hogging the kudos and laying blame on others.

Toot Your Own Horn

If your mummy stays mum about who deserves the credit for the best ideas but blabs when he thinks you deserve the blame, then you have to start getting the word out yourself when you have a good idea. There are ways. You can copy your boss's boss on e-mails with your ideas. You can hold your creative thoughts to yourself until there are higher-ups around ιο witness them coming out your mouth. In other words, you may become a species of mummy yourself, holding your tongue until speaking suits your purpose. This could be a good skill to learn, especially if you have been in the habit of blurting out your thoughts. Being judicious in your communications is a good idea, but be forewarned: a mummy boss who forces you into aping her behavior may be dangerous to your career. She worries that you will outshine her. You take steps to make sure you do. Her worst fears are confirmed—that you are disloyal and trying to take her job away from her. The downward spiral of your relationship speeds up, and in the resulting vortex, your job is the one thing that goes down the drain. Keep your exit strategy handy.

BETTY'S STORY

Betty MacLean had a boss who never said anything unpleasant. If your boss yells and screams negativity around you, Betty's situation may sound heavenly to you. But it has a dark side that drove Betty to the drugstore for more and more antacids. You see, two of the five people who worked on Betty's team goofed off 80 percent of the time. Betty was certain that Wally, her team leader, knew what was going on—he sat in the cube right next to hers. He heard them joking. If she could see the sports Internet sites on their computer screens, so could Wally. He had to notice that only when his boss came into their area did they buckle down and accomplish anything. But Wally stayed mum; he never said a word to them. Betty and one other coworker had to work twice as hard to get everything done, while a couple of jerks never did their fair share and got away with murder. It gave Betty a chronic pain in the top of her stomach.

What could she do to stop this crime against fairness? She could go to Wally and ask him a question. It would be politic to begin with a disclaimer, as in: "Wally, I know that it may be none of my business, but I think somebody needs to make sure everyone here is doing his fair share. Some of us are fielding ten times as many of the calls from the sales force as others. I know some calls are much more complicated than others, but that doesn't account for the people who only pick up if everyone else is busy. Maybe we could make a rule about that?"

Lob It Back into Your Boss's Court

Some bosses seem to expect their people to have ESP. Others think they have already told people things when really they have not. Still others are so afraid to make direct requests that they drop hints about what they want. If the boss is too polite to ask people to do the work, and the staff is too cautious to take the initiative, nothing will get done.

Somehow, the overworked person in a nest of ne'er-do-wells needs to make known to the mummy manager that she sees the problem and that it is the manager's responsibility to deal with it. Be provisional and general, but not too oblique. Be clear about the issue, but leave vague exactly whom you are talking about. If your boss asks you to name names, do not. Instead, say, "I think it would be best if you observed that for yourself."

The Flip Side

Sabrina Williams had the opposite problem—her boss talked too much, blabbing confidential information that affected Sabrina's career trajectory. Sabrina worked for Al in the Human Resources Department of a large Wall Street bank. Al had a Ph.D. in organizational psychology and was generally looked up to as a guru by the management in the company, especially by the other section heads in their department. Sabrina found him entirely sympathetic, especially after she returned from maternity leave. He drew out her feelings about being a working mother. She confessed to him that she sometimes felt guilty about leaving the baby with her sister-in-law Mary. Little Jack was getting good care, and being with his cousins was fine, but she worried that Mary would naturally coddle her own kids more than she did Jack. "Sometimes," she told Al, nearly in tears, "when I am driving to pick him up on my way home, I worry that something awful has happened to him."

In his best supportive psychologist voice, Al reassured Sabrina that lots of young mothers had these misgivings. He said that professionally he knew children were resilient. That being with older children would stimulate little Jack and be good for his development.

Time passed and things seemed to be going okay. Jack certainly was thriving, but Sabrina's career wasn't. It seemed to have stalled. She applied for a posted job as the HR coordinator for the Branch Banking Department. Her friend Doris worked for the department head and thought it would be stimulating and interesting for Sabrina to make the change. She would also get a promotion and more pay, and a chance to work directly with Doris.

A Rude Awakening

When she did not get the job, she asked Doris why. Doris hemmed and hawed about confidentiality, but after Sabrina persisted and swore she wouldn't do anything with the information, Doris revealed that Al had not recommended her. "He told my boss that you were not well adjusted to your role as a working mother. That because you are conflicted, you might make bad decisions about other working mothers or people who had no children. Basically, he painted you as an emotional basket case."

"But, I'm not, am I?" Sabrina protested.

"Of course not," Doris said. "If you ask me, he doesn't want to lose you from his group."

It took a little while, but eventually Sabrina realized that her career chances at that bank had died when Al started to spread the word of his assessment of her personal problems.

Her sister-in-law Mary was 100 percent sure that what Al was doing violated the ethics of his profession, but Sabrina did not see any way to combat him on those grounds. "What good would it do for me to even try? The more I protest that I am not crazy, the more they will think I am." She took her career ambitions elsewhere.

When Mum Is Good

Sometimes being a mummy yourself is the best course of business action. No matter how sympathetic you think he is, be careful what you tell your boss about yourself. Mutual trust and respect with one's colleagues is a beautiful thing. But there are personal matters you are better off keeping to yourself. Only a fiend would have used Sabrina's misgivings against her. Still, prudence dictates that you not put weapons in the hands of monsters who could turn them on you.

When to Surrender

Incompetence in communication is the worst flaw a boss can have. Only through open and productive communication can employees understand what needs to be done so they can contribute to the organization's goals and earn the rewards they work for. If your boss cannot use words to inform, inspire, or persuade, how can he generate enthusiasm for the work, maintain employee motivation, or promote staff development. A boss who cannot—or will not—communicate is a menace. At the very least, working under such a person means you learn nothing, which stalls your career. Bosses who do not lead you to success are leading you over a career cliff. Look elsewhere.

13

THE GIANT SQUID
SEXUAL HARASSMENT

An enormous tentacled creature dwells 3,000 feet down in the inky depths of the ocean. Long thought to be mythical, this elusive cephalopod was photographed by Japanese researchers for the first time in September 2004.

Rosemary Strobach's boss hit on her only once. They were going over reports when Pete gave her an inquiring look. "Karen tells me that you broke up with your boyfriend," he said.

Rosemary was surprised by his interest in her personal life and assumed he was concerned that she might not be able to focus on her job. "Yes. But don't worry. I am not all that brokenhearted. It won't affect my work. It was simply time for us to part. I'm not going to go all dramatic about it."

Pete continued to look at Rosemary with a questioning expression—one she had never seen on his face before. He put down the spreadsheet they had been discussing. "I am interested in you," he said. "I would like us to get together." He said it gently. He didn't try to touch her.

Stunned by his proposal, it took Rosemary a minute to answer. "Gee," was all she could say at first. Finally, she was able to blurt out "I don't think that's something I ought to do."

Pete fixed her with a suggestive gaze. "Ought to or want to?"

"I like working with you" she said. "I just think we should leave it at that. I have always thought it best to keep my work life and my private life separate."

He didn't press his case. Nevertheless, Rosemary left feeling awkward about the whole episode.

When three weeks went by and her boss never brought it up again, she hoped it would pass and be forgotten. She did her best to act natural around him, but that was really hard. Then, about a month later, she was having lunch with Marjorie from accounting, when Marjorie said, "So tell me about your new boyfriend. Or should I say boyfriends?"

Rosemary nearly choked on her tuna sandwich. "I broke up with Manny. You know that."

"Yeah," Marjorie said. "And you never said anything about dating again, but Kevin Hampton told me that Pete told him that you were really going to town with a lot of guys since you left Manny."

Then Rosemary did choke. "He what?" She had to hear Marjorie say it again to believe it.

In the ensuing weeks, she went through all kinds of emotional hell. Guys all over the company—married or not—started asking her out. Some of them raised their eyebrows mimicking a cartoon version of a lothario. They all believed the gossip and expected her to run right out to the local no-tell motel with them.

Rosemary stated having migraines. She woke up at three every morning. She couldn't stop thinking about the rumor mill. Eventually she summoned the courage to confront Pete. "Why are you lying to people about me?"

He gave her a level look and shrugged. "I don't know what you are talking about," he said in a flat, businesslike voice. "Whatever is going on with you, I have to tell you that it is affecting your work. You are looking pretty worn out from what you are doing on your personal time. If you put your social life before the job, you aren't going to last long around here."

A week later she quit. Another option would have been to report Pete for sexual harassment, but Rosemary never thought of what happened to her that way—at least not at the time. She thought sexual harassment meant that your boss tried to force himself on you.

But make no mistake, what Pete did was undeniably sexual harassment. He asked Rosemary out, and when she refused him, he made her life miserable. This could happen to you anywhere in life, but if it happens on the job, it's against the law.

Identifying Squid Behavior

The Giant Squid has been called the poster child for a sea monster. Too bad that other "tentacled monster"—the sexually abusive boss—isn't as rare and elusive. Unfortunately, this poster child for this vilest of office monsters is all too common.

Studies over decades have consistently shown that millions of Americans have experienced sexual harassment. As a result, they suffer physical and emotional maladies, including headaches, depression, high blood pressure, and ulcers. When they refuse their boss's sexual overtures, they are denied raises or promotions; and some bosses find a way to fire the person they feel spurned them.

These slimy squid bosses may tell mortifying dirty jokes, make suggestive remarks, or brush against employees "accidentally." Others make more serious and overt demands and threats.

Why They Do It

Focusing on sexual harassment, I am sure there are volumes written on why people do such things. Ordinarily in these chapters, we try to understand the monster boss's motivations in order to deal with them more intelligently. For this chapter, we aren't going to try to psych out the whys behind this boss's cheesy behavior. Whatever else it is, we are going to treat sexual harassment on the job as what it always is: a power play. We aren't going to waste our time trying to understand Squid bosses. We are going to aim at stopping them. Period.

Corporate Reality

All large companies and many midsize and small ones have policies against sexual harassment. You may have a Human Resources manual that states unequivocally that the company will not tolerate this sort of behavior from its managers. But that does not mean it isn't happening to you or that it will be easy for you to act against the monster who is trying to take advantage of you.

Some corporate policies are lip service, there because of laws on the books. Top management is sometimes not really behind them. Then again, in complex organizations the top managers may be 100 percent sincere, but your boss may be operating in an obscure corner of the corporate structure where his dastardly deeds go unnoticed.

Also, of course, the more powerful your boss—the more clout he has with higher-ups—the more difficult it will be to make trouble for him, no matter how much trouble he is making for you. You need to think through your options and focus your energies on what will work in your circumstances.

It will take courage to fight this beast—there is no doubt about that. To right this wrong you may have to describe your boss's behavior to a complete stranger. Just bringing up the subject may be extremely embarrassing. Quoting words he said, describing gestures he made may make you feel dirty. We have to be ready for you to overcome your natural reticence and make your statements honestly and openly.

Strategies for Coping with Squid Behavior

It is best to take action immediately to stop any form of sexual harassment. There is a clear and uncomplicated way to handle sexual harassment that works in most cases. More than likely, if you follow this procedure, you will take care of your problem.

Speak Up Forcefully

First, tell the boss to stop. Be direct and clear. You may be so embarrassed by what the boss is doing that it leaves you speechless. He probably counts on the shock value of his actions to get the better of you. Nip this behavior in the bud. Otherwise it will only get worse.

If, in your case, this has been going on for a while, don't think it's too late to stop it. If his antics have caught you by surprise in the past, do not be angry with yourself for not responding properly then. Often, when a boss first starts in with the off-color jokes, the unwanted sexual overtures, the pinches, employees are so shocked and upset by the boss's behavior that they can't respond properly. If this is your case, you can still speak up. Preface your first remarks by saying something like, "Steve, I know I have ignored and tried to laugh off what you've been doing, but only because I was too embarrassed to say anything. But it's gone too far for too long."

Some people use humor to put the boss off. This might work, but you risk giving your boss the impression that you think this is a laughing matter. It's not. Better to make your objections serious. Tell him just what it is that you dislike. "Steve, I do not want you to touch me. Please do not do it any more." Or "Richard, I know you find those stories amusing, but I find them embarrassing. Please don't tell them in front of me."

Put It in Writing

If telling an errant boss to cease sexually offensive behavior doesn't make him stop, write him an e-mail or a memo spelling out what you want to happen. Again be straightforward. Talk about the future, not the past. It is not necessary at this point to document what the boss has done to offend you, but you should be clear about what you do—and do not—want to happen in the future. If your company has a written policy dealing with sexual harassment, attach a copy. Send the e-mail or the printed note to the boss. Keep a copy.

Document It

If he persists, keep a log of what he does. Continue to remind him that his behaviors are out of line—that you have asked him politely to stop. Include in your log the date, time, and place of the offensive behavior. Include a description of what he said or did. If others heard or saw, write down their names. At the same time, start documenting your work performance. These slimy octopi might fight back by attacking the quality of your work. You have to have your defenses ready.

Seek Allies

Your next step should be to enlist the support of others. If you suspect that your coworkers are experiencing the same problem, you may want to get them to adopt the same procedures. That way, if your evidence is questioned, you have others who can corroborate your story.

Report Him

Go to HR or your boss's boss with your grievance. All companies have, or should have, written and distributed policies against sexual harassment, and they are legally bound to enforce them. The people you complain to must take you seriously. If they do not, you have every right to take legal action. States and sometimes cities have agencies that handle these kinds of complaints. Find out what agency in your city or county enforces these laws and go to them.

You do not have to suffer. You do not have to remain silent. And you do not have to sacrifice your career to your virtue or your virtue to your career.

Never Use These Rules Dishonestly

The rules against sexual harassment are on the books to protect people. They must never be used to make points or to falsely accuse a person for personal gain. Let me illustrate: Brenda worked as a stockbroker for a firm that asked her to sign a noncompete agreement. Basically, the agreement stated that if she left the firm, she would not work as a broker for another company for two years. Firms do this in order to protect themselves from their employees moving to another job and taking their clients with them. It actually is not much of a deterrent, and there are lawyers prepared to help employees break such promises. The problem is that usually the brokers may be owed commissions when they leave a firm, and lawyers usually advise that giving up the commissions owed is the price of getting out of the noncompete agreement. But Brenda did not like giving up anything. When her lawyer advised her to forfeit her last month's commissions, she found herself another lawyer. This one offered her a way to scare her old company into paying her. He advised that she accuse her former boss of sexual harassment. Her boss, in fact, had done nothing of the sort. "My new lawyer says," she said, "that if he treated me differently in any way because I am a woman that that's a form of sexual harassment. Well, he did treat me differently."

"How?"

"Lots of ways."

She would never say that he had done any of the explicit things that most people would consider actual harassment. In fact, up until the point where the lawyer told her to accuse her boss of sexual harassment, she had never complained about him in any way. Everything she said about him before that made him sound like a decent guy. She wanted a new job because she believed the new firm would put her on a faster track to a partnership. Her accusation was about getting money, not about redressing a real harm.

This is heinous. Many, many people suffer actual torment from their bosses. That anyone would use the specious claim of sexual harassment to win a point, to get money, is a travesty of our laws. If people manipulate the rules, if they lie and cheat, then no one will be believed when they cry "foul." Misusing this law weakens it. If people regularly make false accusations, officials and the general public will not see the need to enforce the law. Then there will be no protection for real victims when they complain that some slimy squid is harassing them.

When to Surrender
NEVER!

14

ARGUS

THE MICROMANAGER

"Now Argus had a hundred eyes in his head, and never went to
sleep with more than two at a time, so that he kept watch of Io
constantly."
Bullfinch's Mythology

Neil Robinson worked for a small events-planning business.
When conventions came to Chicago, they staged parties for
participating companies—especially companies from out of
town that needed a lot of help arranging entertainment for
clients. Neil liked his job, and at first he admired Peggy, the
founder and owner of the company—admired her a great
deal. Their work required enormous attention to detail. One
little typo in the date of an event for instance, could mean
that a party room was reserved for a Tuesday instead of a
Wednesday—a mistake like that could spell disaster—and
cost a lot of money, especially when guarantees were involved.
So it did not surprise or upset Neil at all when Peggy checked
and rechecked every detail of their arrangements, especially
when he was new on the job.

As Neil gained experience, though, he began to see Peggy's constant double-checking as compulsive and destructive.
She not only micromanaged the important details, she also

kept her Argus eyes on every single speck of minutiae in the company. "What a control freak," Neil said. "I wouldn't be surprised if she counted the leaves on the fichus tree before going home each night, and again in the morning, and threw a fit if one was missing."

Worst of all, Peggy sat in the middle of the office and listened in on Neil's side of phone calls—with clients, with catering managers at hotels, with anyone and everyone. When he got off the phone, she frequently corrected what he had said, or offered "helpful" suggestions for how to handle such a call in the future. He wasn't a trainee anymore. He knew what to say. Nevertheless, she kept it up, even if she had nothing substantive to say. It drove him nuts. He couldn't concentrate on what the person on the other end of the line was saying. Whenever he picked up the phone, all he could think about was Peggy's ears, two feet away on the other side of the divider. Distracted and self-conscious, he had trouble keeping up his end of the conversation. He stumbled over his words and sounded incompetent, which only made her "corrections" worse.

He was ready to explode. But he bit his tongue. For way too long. Until one day, when Peggy started coaching him during a conversation with a client. He was trying to discuss how the client wanted to arrange seating at a dinner party. Peggy's voice came over the divider—"make sure you get the seating chart. Make sure it has first and last names. Make sure we have proper spelling." Neil never said another word. He hung up on the client, stood up, and walked out and never went back.

Corporate Reality

Well-run companies are, for the most part, going in the opposite direction to Peggy's obsessive-compulsive, micro-management style. Instead, they are giving employees more and more freedom to be creative and invent their own solutions to problems.

But there are still those compulsive supervisors who never shut all 100 of their eyes. They stand around and gape, demand constant reporting, and insist on correcting inconsequential mistakes. They just cannot resist telling you how to do what you already know backwards and forwards. Nothing seems to get under employees skins like managers who hover.

These Argus bosses usually get into their management jobs because company managements see their obsession with control as a useful skill in overseeing lower-level functions where controlling costs or getting the details right is crucial. In large corporations, however, these minutia moguls usually never rise above the first levels of management. They never qualify for the bigger jobs because they cannot focus on the big picture, so fixated are they by the tiny issues they are compelled to control. Small may be beautiful in some contexts, but not when "tiny" is applied to minds and concerns.

The most ambitious micromanagers, who succeed in companies because of their attention to detail, easily become frustrated with their lack of progress above the level of first-line supervision. Many of these start their own businesses. Here, too, their futures are frequently stunted. Their companies may survive and even produce decent profits, but they seldom grow to any size because the founder is unable to let go of total control. The size of their organizations is limited by the span of their personal control.

Strategies for Coping with Argus Behavior

In the myth of Argus, the giant with the 100 eyes, the god Mercury contrived to put the beast to sleep by telling him long, long stories. Employees of micromanagers may be able to put their bosses at ease—close all of their ever-watchful eyes—by giving them oceans of information, reporting on their activities, so that the boss will not have to ask. Try it. It might work. If your boss lacks a bit of confidence in himself or in you, a nice security blanket of information might put his fears to rest. But if your boss is truly compulsive, you may, like Mercury, find that you can put 98 of his eyes to sleep, but he will still keep 2 open. Many supervisors who attend to every minute detail have diagnosable personality disorders. There is not going to be much you can do to put them at ease. If you cannot stand the constant vigilance, you may have to hit the street.

In Neil's case, he put up with Peggy's interfering until he couldn't stand it anymore. Considering the state he must have been in, getting up and walking out was understandable, and from the point of view of his mental and physical health, might have been the best action to take at that moment, but this is not necessarily the best strategy for managing his career. He should never have let things go on for so long that he came to that point. When Peggy's behavior first began to bother him, *before* his nerve endings were so raw with fretting, he might have asked her not to micromanage him. Not that it would have worked, but he could have tried. Then, if Peggy didn't lay off, he should have exited gracefully.

Putting off dealing with work problems will only stunt your career growth. Too many people do what Neil did— they do not nip difficulties in the bud; they wait until they blossom into blooming hatred and rage, and then they do something precipitous, like quitting on the spot. And nothing seems to enrage people like micromanagement. Do yourself a favor. Speak up before you explode.

The Special Case of Electronic Surveillance

Some Argus-eyed managers have found ways to extend what they can oversee. They have embraced electronics in a big way. Every year more companies employ high-tech monitoring to watch what's going on at work. Ninety-two percent of American corporations report that they use surveillance equipment of one sort or another. Given these statistics, chances are the boss is using it to watch you. Monstrous bosses use it to spy on their employees in secret and astoundingly disgusting ways. You may be one of the many employees who have little or no privacy at work. His snooping may follow you home, to the doctor's office, to the bar where you thought you were just hanging out with your friends.

There is widespread use of hidden cameras in workplaces. Security cameras in stairwells and parking garages keep us all safe. Fine, but voyeurs put them where they should never go—in bathrooms, locker rooms, places where employees undress. Some bosses videotape from these cameras. And they get away with it. Not surprisingly, women employees are more likely to be videotaped in the bathroom. What possible business purpose could this serve? And yet, as of this writing, only three states—New York, California, and Rhode Island—have laws against employers videotaping employees in places where they undress. Only two—Connecticut and Delaware—make it compulsory for companies to tell employees that they are under surveillance. In one court case, employees sued their boss who had used peepholes to spy on women in the bathroom! This is bizarre and highly offensive, but still the court sided with the employer. Your boss has a right to supervise your work, he has absolutely no right to see—and record!—you naked.

As cheap and easy as it is to acquire and install cameras, more and more employers employ electronic monitoring. The more common such equipment becomes, the more likely some monster will abuse it. Almost all companies—80 percent in one survey—tell their employees that they are under surveillance. But mind the gap. Ninety-two percent of companies use the equipment, and only 80 percent tell their employees what they are doing. That means that 12 percent watch on the sly. These companies employ millions of people who have no idea that the clock on the wall or the mirror in the locker room might hide a camera.

Watch Your Keystrokes

Like video cameras, computer-monitoring software has legitimate business purposes. Employers want to keep track of whether employees—especially telecommuters are actually at work. They use keyboard-monitoring software to count keystrokes or monitor whether the person is at the computer at all. The number of keystrokes you enter per minute may be the measure by which you are evaluated. Sometimes standards are set pretty high—in which case, employees can fall victim to stress disabilities and painful ailments such as carpal tunnel syndrome. To protect yourself, no matter what standard your boss sets, watch out for pain and stress that doesn't go away. Do your job with diligence. But allowing yourself to become disabled by repetitive-motion syndrome will not help your career. Talk to the boss if the demand becomes so much it could injure you. Do it before you are wearing a brace and popping painkillers.

Watch Your Internet Use

Your company may also use one or more of the evolving kinds of software packages on the market to monitor your e-mail and what Web sites you visit when you are on the company computer network. This situation is tricky. Certainly employers have a right to make rules about employees writing personal e-mails, buying books on the Internet, or making personal phone calls during business hours. Most companies have policies restricting such activities, but almost none strictly forbid it. This seems only fair. As Chapter 10 describes, the lines between work and home are blurring—with cell phones, BlackBerrys, and telecommuting. If the boss expects you to field calls from customers or finish up a report on your "free" time, she also has to expect that, while at work, you will take an occasional call from your aged auntie or go online to buy party favors for your daughter's Sweet Sixteen. If your Argus expects the former, but doesn't allow the latter, you may need to respectfully remind her that the company cannot have it both ways.

Most likely, all you can do about this surveillance is be aware of it. Be judicious about what you do. For instance, do not imagine that because you delete the e-mails and empty your deleted items folder, that what you wrote is gone forever. Most systems keep copies of everything, so you can never be sure your messages are actually gone. This software might have been installed in your computer without your ever knowing it's there. For your privacy protection, do not use the company computer to send information you do not want known about yourself—not even from your own private e-mail account. The same goes for the content of private phone calls. Big Brother may be listening. Some companies even "backup" the voice mail systems and listen to messages left for you on your office voice mail. The lack of laws and regulations to govern this type of snooping leave employers free rein.

CHARLIE'S STORY

Charlie Bing found out the hard way that using the office telephone for private calls was not really private. In fact, the sporting goods store that he managed had a published policy that said employees who worked in the office could make a "reasonable" number of personal calls. One day a friend called Charlie to tell him about a job opportunity in another company. Charlie was interested. What he didn't know was that the company, having experienced an unusual amount of theft from his store, suspected an "inside job" and was recording his calls. They did not get evidence against him for theft, but they fired him on the basis that he was "looking" for another job. Charlie sued for invasion of privacy based on the company's published policy allowing personal calls. He lost.

Protect Your Privacy

Regarding phone surveillance, did you know that your company cell phone, your company vehicle, maybe even your employee ID card can tell your boss where you are within a few yards.

The GPS on your cell phone is there to help 911 responders find you in an emergency. This is how the police locate people lost in the woods, which is great. But companies also use GPS to monitor employees. Your boss may be tracking you using your business cell phone, and not just where you were, but how long you stayed there. As long as the phone is on, the company might be keeping track of you, even during off hours. It's one thing for companies to use the technology available to make their workers more efficient, to gather work-related intelligence, but it is unsavory for them monitor their private lives twenty-four/seven.

The law allows employers to demand that you take a drug test, even if there is no reason to suspect you are a user. Sixty-two percent of employers conduct some form of workplace drug testing. Companies also employ undercover detectives to investigate vandalism, theft, or drug use, but in the process these gumshoes may also report on employees' private health, family, or sex lives. They sometimes snoop not only on your employer's premises, but also after hours—wherever you go.

Are there laws to protect you? Yes and no. Mostly no. As noted, very few states specifically forbid employer surveillance of employees. And when workers try to use the privacy laws to redress these grievances, the courts almost always side with the employers.

Employers should be monitoring only work-related activities. They should use the GPS on your phone or vehicle to make sure of your work, not your social or family life. Most employers actually do what is right in this regard and tell their employees that they are under surveillance. Some try, as all should, to do this with minimum intrusiveness and use it for management, not to find transgressions for which they then punish you.

If your company doesn't let you know what monitoring they use, it is fair for you to ask. In any case, make no assumptions that you have privacy on the job. These statistics should forewarn you:

- Percentage of companies that have fired workers for misusing the Internet: 26 percent
- Percentage of companies that have terminated employees for misusing e-mail: 25 percent
- Percentage of companies that have fired employees for misusing the office phones: 6 percent
- Percentage of companies that monitor workers' Web site connections: 76 percent
- Percentage of employers that track content, keystrokes, and time spent at the keyboard: 36 percent
- Percentage of employers that store and review employees' computer files: 55 percent
- Percentage of employers that have had employee e-mails subpoenaed by courts and regulatory agencies: 20 percent
- Percentage of employers who monitor how much time employees spend on the telephone and track what numbers they call: 51 percent
- Percentage of companies that use GPS to track employees' mobile phones: 5 percent
- Percentage of companies that use GPS to track company vehicles: 8 percent
- Percentage of companies that use it to monitor employee ID/Smartcards: 8 percent

All of these numbers are increasing. Find out if it's happening to you. If they will not tell you, assume they are watching you.

15

CUJO
GREED AND ARROGANCE THAT
RUINS THE WHOLE COMPANY

Stephen King's title character, Cujo, starts out as a cute puppy.
Instead of man's best friend, after being bitten by a rabid bat, the
dog turns into a satanic killer.

A classic example of this danger centers on the *Challenger*
disaster in the 1980s and the plight of an engineer who tried
to get NASA to postpone the launch of the ill-fated shuttle.
He feared the cold temperatures in Florida that January
would cause *Challenger*'s O-rings to fail. "I fought like hell to
stop that launch," he said. His management sent him, his fellow engineers, and their data away, saying—as reported on
National Public Radio—that whether to launch had to be "a
management decision."

He said he prayed as he watched the launch and wept
when it exploded and seven people died needlessly. He
blamed himself "for not insisting." Investigators blamed an
excess of NASA's gung-ho, can-do attitude.

They called the same problem "launch fever" when, years
later, *Columbia*, *Challenger*'s sister ship, burned up on reentry,

killing another seven astronauts. The *New York Times* reported that while *Columbia* was still in orbit, another engineer, Rodney Rocha, watched over and over again for hours the taped images of foam breaking away from Columbia's fuel tanks on launch. He feared potentially fatal damage. All he wanted was more data—to get outside help to look at the shuttle's wing, to make sure. If NASA found a problem, they could try to mount a rescue. He and his fellow engineers wanted astronauts aboard *Columbia* or spy satellites or powerful telescopes on the ground to look at the wing and give them information to properly assess the damage.

In response, his management made references to "Chicken Little" and, according to the *New York Times*, "hotly" resisted the engineers.

Rocha tried repeatedly to overcome managerial resistance. He sent e-mails, one in boldface asking if they could "petition (beg)" for help getting the images that would let them see the extent of the damage. Rocha's pleas hit a brick wall on a dead-end street. *Columbia*'s flight director wrote an e-mail saying, "I consider it a dead issue."

Rocha felt he had no choice but to give up. He and his fellow engineers had been told as a matter of policy not to go over their bosses' heads. Without support, he lost his determination to get the data that might have saved lives. He had no drive left to continue the fight. The morning of the disaster, as he watched data coming in from *Columbia*'s heat sensors, Rocha called his wife and asked her to pray.

There is nothing wrong with prayer, but when engineers who are capable of and actually practice rocket science have to resort to it as their one weapon against managerial intransigence, disaster is the outcome. It wasn't just Rodney Rocha's "issue" that died, so did the seven astronauts he tried so hard to save.

Identifying Cujo Behavior

When he wrote *Cujo*, Stephen King chose a St. Bernard for his killer dog—upping the irony. St. Bernards were bred in the mountains of Switzerland to rescue travelers caught in blizzards in the high, remote passes. Of all canines, they should be the most responsible and beneficent. But Cujo kills. The perfect metaphor for a top executive who destroys the organization he is charged to protect. Rabies at the top leads to sickness throughout the organization.

Two possible sicknesses infect our would-be protective watchdogs, turning them into predatory curs: arrogance and greed.

Arrogance first. Executive egotism stops the flow of the lifeblood of organizations. No, I'm not talking about money. The truth is subtler than money. Information. The flow of information is what nourishes the corporate brainpower, keeps its limbs supple and its muscles strong, keeps it from tipping or, in a spasm of ignorance, throwing itself off a cliff. The corporate heart pumps it. Heartless organizations preclude its circulation.

Some organizations make it nearly impossible for unpopular information to be communicated to the top. When the truth might upset the most powerful people around, we bury it.

Arrogance is bad enough. Greed is even more repulsive. All you have to say is one word—Enron. All those employees following their leaders ninety miles an hour off a cliff—one or two questioning, the others too busy admiring their bank balances to watch where they are going. They complied, not to say colluded, until the fiasco was too far gone to stop, and their own futures crashed with the company.

From *Never Work for a Jerk*, my previous book on this subject: "Be skeptical about any company that forgets about the basics and tries to make its money by financial manipulation. The only healthy ways for an organization to succeed financially are through constant innovation or superior customer satisfaction. If your top management doesn't seem to know this, run." Smoke and mirrors cannot create real value.

The vital lesson of the debacle in Houston is that it was not just an economic washout; it was human calamity. The documentaries, the news stories, books, and analyses create a genuine horror movie. Scary. Monstrous even. Twenty thousand Enron employees lost their jobs. So did another twenty-nine thousand people at Arthur Anderson, the company's accounting firm, some of whose members tried to cover up the fraud. Two billion dollars in pension and retirement funds evaporated. Tragically, John C. Baxter, an Enron executive, committed suicide. He said the stain of what they had done would "never wear off." It took Enron sixteen years to build up and only twenty-four days to go bankrupt. Pride, arrogance, and greed drove it off the cliff.

Cujo is the perfect name for fiend-instead-of-friend CEOs who eat the corporate assets they are paid, often exorbitantly, to preserve. They neglect their employees' and stockholders' interests. The company's future is strangled. The only thing that matters to these curs is self-aggrandizement.

Fat Cats

The ostentation of rabid CEOs is legendary. Thousands spent on haircuts and shower curtains. Companies paying for parking fees, country club memberships, use of the company jet, private school tuition, multimillion-dollar birthday parties for spouses and children, Manhattan apartments, NBA season tickets. These are standard tabloid stories, repeated so often they lose their shock value.

Imagine if you did not have to pay for any of these things. Who wouldn't want to get all this free with salary and normal benefits and bonuses that top $100 million as a year-end extra? These are among the perks corporate CEOs collect, often while running their companies into the ground.

No amount of pubic ridicule seems to deter the Cujo CEOs; no excess is too wretched, no expenditures too shaming. Greed is the rabid bat that has bitten them, and they seem as sick as the 200-pound former puppy who now skulks in wait for any tidbit he can sink his hungry teeth into.

Tax and reporting rules allow these executives, and their boards that approve these arrangements, to keep them quiet. The executive perk pie is cut up into little pieces and hidden here and there in the books. Most of the worst excesses have come out only after the companies went bankrupt or, famously, in divorce proceedings, where displaced wives demanded a share of the perks in their alimony settlements.

Where's J.P. When We Need Him?

It begins not with perks. They are icing on the corporate cake. It starts with huge compensation packages. Banker J. P. Morgan said he would never lend money to any company where the highest-paid executive got more than twenty times the salary of the lowest-paid employee. Hardly anyone would tag that old robber baron as a bleeding-heart champion of the common man. With this thinking, J.P. was looking out for himself, worried about what kinds of bets his bank should lay on corporate loans. Overpaid executives were a symptom of risks he wasn't willing to take. If the top people took too much for themselves, they were not looking out for the future of the company.

A company without a secure future cannot repay its loans. No one would argue the fact that it is difficult to run a huge organization and that the people who take that responsibility should be well paid for their efforts. But how much is too much? A company with greedy executives looked like a bad bet for J. P. Morgan; it's a worse bet for its employees.

In the United States today, in *Fortune* 500 companies, the average CEO earns four hundred times the salary of the average of all the people below him in the organizational chart.

Four hundred times, not J.P. Morgan's twenty. And that's the average of *all* the people, not the lowest-paid worker, as in J. P. Morgan's formula. That is to say that the average CEO makes more in a day than the average of everybody else's salary for a whole year. Old J.P. would not be making many loans to today's top American corporations.

Corporate Reality

If you look abroad at executive pay, you often find a different story. One study, comparing the relative compensation for CEOs in comparable companies at home and abroad, found that American CEOs make six to twenty times as much as their counterparts in other countries.

In the United States, the distribution of all corporate goodies is lopsided. With stock options, for instance, in a typical company 75 percent of the options go to CEOs, 15 percent to the next fifty highest-compensated executives, and only 10 percent to all other employees. And although in recent years productivity has increased by 65 percent, median family income has risen only 22 percent. While CEO pay and corporate profits have increased, the buying power of the average family has gone down.

The worst of the greedy forget about ethics and about their business's success. Their personal measure of their performance is their compensation and perks. They do look at the stock price, but mostly because it is tied to their bonuses and options.

Who's on Board?

Aren't boards of directors supposed to control this sort of thing? Yes. Board members should be the guardians who oversee businesses and make sure they are managed properly. They ostensibly provide direction, establish goals, set strategies, and assign priorities. They act as advisors, help the management create a strong organization, and motivate the workforce. Their legal and fiduciary responsibilities include guiding the organization to accomplish its mission and protecting its assets. In other words, they are supposed to function as a whole pack of shepherds and guard dogs.

Researchers have found that the boards of the most successful companies do not look for excuses and blame others. They do not kick butts and take names. They provide wisdom and perspective and deliver returns to shareholders by making sure the companies deliver top-notch goods and services to their customers.

Monster boards, however, have been implicated in a number of the scandals. The most frequent complaint is that they rubber-stamp unconscionable compensation packages for CEOs. But sometimes, in the sale of a company, they look out for themselves and not the company and shareholders. In one case, a board took a $21 billion offer over a $26 billion buyout price. Why would they decide to take so much less? Because the lower bidder indemnified them against penalties and fines associated with criminal and regulatory probes into alleged malfeasance on their parts. Needless to say the stockholders were not pleased to accept $5 billion (with a *B*) less for their company, just to keep the board members out of jail or from paying fines.

Strategies for Coping with Cujo

As children, we learn from our families the art of fitting in, of belonging to a group. In every group we join, we pay the price of membership. To be valued by the other members, we respect the rules, pay attention to the things the group values, and ignore the things it ignores. We buy the cozy feeling of acceptance by filtering out information the group prefers to deny, by not asking embarrassing questions. Eventually, we start to think the way the group thinks.

Choose Carefully

Be very careful what group you join. Once you are in, you will feel the pressure to conform. You will start to rationalize the way you think and act. If your organization starts down the wrong road, will you find the courage to communicate the information that may save your company from disaster? Even if you try, will your management listen? If arrogance has turned your shepherd's, your watchdog's fervor into fever, your managers will reject your warnings, or punish you for trying to communicate them.

Keep Your Eyes and Ears Open

How can we protect ourselves from greedy grabs and unconscionable arrogance at the top? We cannot march into the executive suite shouting "Oink, oink" at the piggies there. But nor do we have to sit still and watch them rob us of our future.

It can be very hard to tell when the company is foundering because of top executive betrayal. Just days before the debacle, Kenneth Lay told the Enron staff, "The company is in the best shape it has ever been in." Wall Street analysts can love corporations that are a house of cards. Lawyers and accountants may cover for them. In 2000, Enron's board received kudos when their firm was rated one of five best-governed corporations in the United States.

There are, however, some telltale signs that can warn you that there is something rotten in the corporate kingdom. Here are some things to watch out for.

Stock Price That Contradicts Management Claims

If your management tells everyone all is well but the stock price is falling for no apparent reason, somebody is selling shares. Maybe it's someone who knows something. Maybe it is the very people at the top who are reassuring you. Knowing that disaster is around the next bend, perhaps they have decided to dump their stock before the truth gets out.

Profits No One Can Understand

These are often attributed to the "magic of the marketplace." More likely you are looking at "that old black magic." If your top management declares huge successes that are unexplainable by normal means, either the accomplishments do not exist or they were not gotten by normal, that is to say, honest, means. Imaginary profits that lead to multimillion-dollar bonuses may come just before the "restatement of earnings" puts the whole company in bankruptcy court.

Earnings Put Before Scruples

Be on your guard at the first whiff that your corporate leaders play fast and loose with what's right. For short periods, companies can get away with producing shoddy products, flouting environmental laws, or slithering around SEC rules. When they get caught, it costs. All too frequently it costs the employees their jobs.

Two Sets of Books

Unless you are in the top rungs of the accounting department, you probably will not know if your company is keeping two sets of books. If you do, what are you doing there?

Top Executives Who Constantly Fight Regulations

No doubt overregulation cramps the corporate style, but most regulations are put in place to right real wrongs or stop harmful practices. If your management despises reasonable regulation, think about what freedoms they seek. Is what they want permission to do really in everyone's best interest? When Kenneth Lay fought the government to allow Enron more leeway in its operations, he won. What was removed was not a barrier to corporate prosperity but the guardrail protecting a hairpin turn on the economic highway.

Dog-Eat-Dog Corporate Culture

Working in an environment that encourages employees to step on one another cannot be pleasant for you. Even if you are winning at the moment, think about it. If you rise in your company by winning pitched dog-eat-dog battles, the people at the top must be the most vicious of the cannibals. That alone should scare you away, even if your own conscience is in a coma.

People Who Used to Care Quit

When middle managers and important innovators who cared passionately about the mission of the company start for the door, you may want to consider falling into step behind them.

A Sudden Flurry of Resignations at the Top

If you stay long enough to see this, it's probably too late to do anything. This is usually the last indicator of impending disaster, just before the proverbial hits the fan. Remember how fast that titanic ship Enron sank. If you ignore the warnings above, you may wind up below when your corporate craft goes down.

When to Surrender

You may not be able to stop that greedy, nefarious, or arrogant corporate Cujo. Corporations are dictatorships, not democracies. But you can vote with your feet. Do not stick around until they order you to shred the evidence.

16

THE BLAIR WITCH
THE REAL PROBLEM IS YOU

Four young filmmakers invented the legend of the Blair Witch and showed how imagined monsters can terrify, without gore, without blood, with nothing but an expectation of atrocity.

Joanne Williamson graduated with a degree in art history and headed for New York, with a dream of working in one of its legendary art galleries. Qualified, attractive, personable, she soon landed a job that she bragged about to her friends. Everything was perfect, especially her boss, Harrison. He was knowledgeable, had great contacts, and handled talented and successful artists. Upper Madison Avenue was Joanne's top of the world until the boss's flaws began to show.

According to Joanne, Harrison never gave Joanne any credit for her accomplishments. He minimized her contribution to the gallery's sales. He paid her commissions but would never admit to her or anyone else that she was good at what she did.

After less than a year, she gave up and took her skills to another gallery. There her new boss, Naomi, was perfect. This time, Joanne told herself, by working for a woman she would get the respect she deserved. Naomi was elegant and had wonderful taste, but after a few months Joanne began to view her as a philistine. According to Joanne, Naomi wasn't really interested in art. She was far more interested in what she saw framed in the mirror than in what she saw framed in her gallery. "I never met anyone so vain," Joanne grumbled. No use hanging around with that princess, so Joanne moved on after only five months.

Grace owned the next gallery where Joanne landed, but—you guessed it—it wasn't long before Joanne concluded that her new idol had feet of clay. As with the others, Joanne became convinced that Grace wasn't really the warm, genuine art lover she first seemed. According to Joanne, Grace only wanted to own a gallery so she could spend time with rich people, take them to fancy expense-account lunches, and brag about selling paintings for enormous prices to shallow celebrities.

This story went on, but you get the idea. Every job Joanne started seemed wonderful at the beginning but soon became a big disappointment. With her, however, it seems like a combination of things. Joanne loves art. She sees it in as an expression of the spirit of all humanity. Her belief in the spiritual nature of art raises her expectations of her bosses. To her they should not have been ordinary business people earning a living by buying and selling something physical, like paintings and sculptures. They should be priests and priestesses in the temple of art.

This syndrome of impossible expectations affects not only people in the arts, but also people working in humanitarian, nonprofit work. They go to work not just to earn a living and do something useful—they want to save the world. This is a magnificent goal. Certainly people who work toward it are on the side of the angels. But they condemn themselves to utter frustration if they expect their coworkers and their bosses to be those angels.

Identifying Blair Witch Behavior

The Blair Witch Project is not a story about a monster. It is about how emotions churning inside a person can make for a terrifying experience, even if there is no such thing as the monster they imagine. The film opens with a group of people beginning an endeavor with great enthusiasm. It is going to be wonderful. They cannot wait to get started— just like a person beginning a new job. The kids in the film wind up horrified. So it happens on the job, when employees constantly look for something from the boss that bosses should not be asked to give. The employees wind up feeling betrayed. Like Joanne Williamson, a person can go through life repeating this pattern.

Unhappy employees sometimes resent all authority figures. It is difficult to say why, but if you have never had a great relationship with an authority figure—teachers, parents, sergeants—you may find yourself reacting negatively to any pressure to conform. Do you dislike almost all rules and regulations? Do you lose your temper when pushed to do something someone else's way? Do you see criticism of your work, even mild criticism, as idiotic? If you resent all management, you will see all managers in a negative light. Then, when this "lesser human being" judges your work, it will drive you bonkers. If you think you're in the grips of Blair Witch syndrome, ask yourself the following questions:

- Is that person you consider a monster one of a long list of managers who have dreadfully disappointed you?
- With each new job do you think "Finally an authority figure who really understands me?"
- Are your hopes dashed before long?
- What do you expect from a person you would consider a good boss? Emotional support? Admiration? Affirmation that you are worthy, smart, adorable?

- When you do not get what you are looking for, does your disappointment harden into resentment?
- Do you always blame the boss for your failures? Do you never examine how you may have contributed to them?
- When you do not get what you are looking for, does your disappointment harden into resentment?

If you hate your job and it's not the work, not the organizational structure, if you think your failures and disappointments have nothing to do with you, if it's the boss—she's a witch—you could be creating your own monster movie script.

Corporate Reality

Here's a dose of reality: Bosses have authority over their employees. That means they have the right to make decisions about what the employee does, how he does it, how much he is required to do. To exercise that right, the boss must have some power—which to a certain extent gives him the right to control the employee's actions. That power comes from several sources. The company puts the manager in charge of a work unit and says, in effect, this whole organization will abide by your decisions regarding the work for your group. The extreme of this is the military during combat, where traditionally the commanding officer has the right to take the life of any soldier who will not follow orders.

Most modern corporations actually give very little authority to their managers, especially supervisors at the lower levels. In fact, in many cases, bosses have responsibilities without having a commensurate level of authority to carry them out. For instance, it is unusual these days to find a manger who has the sole right to hire and fire employees. If you think about it, in most companies the employees are immune from bosses taking precipitous action against them.

Most bosses' real power comes from their ability to control company resources. They get to decide who gets which projects and who gets to work with which group. Although they usually cannot make decisions unilaterally, they can influence important ones concerning pay and promotions.

It is this power of opinion that is strongest in modern bosses. They have the right to judge our work. Frequently they pass judgment on our character and personality. To the extent that their boss respects their opinion, they have a great deal to say about our future. In a sense, we give them this power over us by taking the job in the first place, and then by wanting the pay raises and promotions the company has to offer.

Perhaps the boss's strongest personal power of opinion comes from our need for the boss's approval. If you need a person's admiration, she has a great deal of control over you. In this case, the employee invests the boss with power by needing her good opinion.

There is a paradox here. Some people empower their bosses by deciding to work for them or by needing their approval and then resent the boss's authority. Then they repeat this process with every boss they ever have.

JOHN'S STORY

John Carr simply could not keep a job. He quarreled with every boss he had. He said they were all stupid. Sometimes he lasted a few months, sometimes only a few days. But sooner or later, he either quit or got fired. His wife was the main wage earner in the family. In the beginning when John lost a job, she commiserated with him. She knew that some bosses were difficult, and that John was a proud person who wouldn't want to be pushed around.

As a result of John's penchant for job hopping, he and his family moved nineteen times in twelve years; his children went to eleven different elementary schools. Over the years, when John came home with complaints about his boss, his wife found it harder and harder to believe that John was right and yet another manager was totally at fault, idiotic, or incompetent. After years of a nomadic existence and constant financial problems, she lost all sympathy for her husband. Finally, when their children were in high school, John's long-suffering wife left him and was at last able to offer her children a modicum of stability. The problem, she was certain, was not in all those bosses, but inside John.

John's case is extreme, but many people have difficulty with authority. They cannot stand anyone having power over them. The very nature of the boss-subordinate relationship rubs them the wrong way. They find it impossible to have someone in charge that that they must answer to. Clearly, John is one of those people.

Strategies for Coping with Blair Witch Behavior

If you have had a number of bosses and blamed them all for your difficulties at work, you need to start examining yourself. Look inside for possible issues with authority and unrealistic expectations.

Be Realistic

Some people get into trouble with authority figures because they have unrealistic expectations of what and who a boss is supposed to be. Some people expect the boss to be the perfect partner or parent they always wanted, who with perfect methods, absolute kindness, and infallible understanding and judgment solves all problems, dispels all insecurities, and makes the employee a happy person. They expect to agree with every decision the boss makes. If you do this, you give the boss too much power because you want his approval so much. You put yourself in a no-win position.

Everyone deserves a sense of satisfaction from work, a feeling of accomplishment, the dignity of making a contribution and earning a living. These satisfactions of basic human needs must be part of your work life as you pursue happiness on the job. But there is a limit to what the boss can do for you.

You must also seek meaningful life experiences elsewhere. If your family life and friendships outside of work do not provide them, try to fix that. And look to volunteer work, study, music, or creative or artistic expression.

Look for Patterns

Often, people who suffer from these false hopes do not even know what they are doing. They see their disillusionments as individual events. Not a pattern. But look again at your work history and try to see if some need inside you has caused a series of bitter disappointments. You need to find a way stop torturing yourself.

Know Your Company Structure

Often employees imagine their immediate boss has much more power than the organization actually gives her. Middle managers, especially first-line supervisors, do not usually make decisions on their own. If you did not get the raise you wanted or the promotion you thought you deserved, it could be that the boss actually decided on the amount, but much more likely, the corporation has rules that severely limited what she could do. Certainly, first-line managers get a lot of grief for decisions made far above them in organizations: like off-shoring jobs or reorganizing departments. It's natural to target those close by, but let's be careful how we choose the lightening rods we zap with our disappointments. Fair is fair, and rational.

Own It

Remember when we discussed Dracula bosses and how they take credit for their employees' accomplishments but blame those under them for any failures? The reverse seems to happen with some employees. Perhaps we all have this tendency. When things are going well we like to take the credit. We say: "I was lucky" or "I was smart" or "I was in the right place at the right time." But when things are going poorly, we look somewhere else to put the blame. We say: "They gave me too much to do" or "He didn't tell me what my priorities should be" or "My boss is a monster."

Since the boss is ostensibly in charge, it is easy for dissatisfied employees to blame her for any work-related problem. Since people spend so much of their waking lives at work, they can easily blame the boss for their general dissatisfaction with life.

People who resent authority chafe under any kind of criticism. Maybe they so lack confidence that they cannot bear to see themselves making mistakes. Whatever the reason, they want to take the credit for all their progress on the job, but blame the boss whenever what they attempt does not come up roses.

Are You Allergic to Authority?

If you are never wrong and your boss frequently is, maybe you better take a look at the yardsticks you use to judge yourself and him.

In some people, these characteristic resentments and difficulties seem intractable parts of their personalities. Why people have such severe problems with authority is a big question. Psychologists cite many possible reasons, all embedded in childhood experiences. They call people who have trouble accepting authority of any kind "counter-dependent." They say these people usually mistrust everyone, are afraid of obligating themselves, are driven to make a personal impact, or have a cynical view of life.

Power evokes strong but mixed emotions in people who resist authority. If you are one of these people, you will be drawn to authority and repelled by it at the same time.

Strangely enough, people with this syndrome of resentment of authority often make very good bosses themselves. They seem to have an instinctive sense of what will motivate others and how to treat people who work for them in a way that will preclude the irritation with authority they so often feel.

Scratching the Itch

If you are allergic to authority figures you need to take some steps to minimize the damage your feelings will do to your career. You need to seek work that will insulate you from the worst of your indignation. Here are some paths that might get you there:

Avoid Authoritarian Bosses

The more collegial and participative your boss, the less likely you are to chafe under his supervision. Before you take a job, ask about the boss's management style. It's tricky to ask a direct question about this. Get at it by asking the boss to describe the typical project in the area and probe about how she and her employees share ideas. Her answers should give you an idea of how closely she supervises and how directive she is in how her employees work as well as what they work on.

Look for a Job in a Company with an Open and Flexible Structure

You may thrive in a loosely organized team structure where you will have leeway to be creative in how you do your job. You will feel less hemmed in, and you may find space to flex your independence. These companies also often employ a team approach to performance appraisal, where your competence and productivity will be evaluated not by one supervisor, but by peers and customers as well. That will give you a range of opinion that will feel fairer and, hopefully, easier to accept.

Look for a Job Where You Can Work Independently

Branch managers in banks, classroom teachers, and FedEx delivery agents do not have their boss's looking over what they do on a constant basis. If you can manage your own performance and hold yourself to excellent standards, you will do better in situations where you are free of constant supervision. The ultimate in this category, of course, is for you to start your own business. Not everyone has the capacity to succeed at her own business, but that high need for independence seems to be one of the drives that makes entrepreneurs successful.

17

THE MONSTER IN YOUR MIRROR
YOU'RE SCARING YOUR EMPLOYEES

The *Sesame Street* celebrity version of the song "Monster in the Mirror" has everyone from Ray Charles to the Simpsons singing "wubba wubba" along with Grover, who croons about how he tamed the monster in the mirror with kindness.

Are you a manager? If you are, before we part company, I want you to ask yourself how your employees might view you. Does your managerial style include a wardrobe of black capes and green goo? Do you fear your employees might see a monster in you? You may be a monster boss's victim and at the same time some other victim's monster boss. If you think this is possible, remain calm. Management is a skill. You can learn it.

Actually Grover's song has a point. In good management practice, kindness is a good place to start.

The Good News

First, be kind to yourself. If you lack the supervisory and managerial skills to motivate, supportively correct and counsel, and inspire your people, it's probably not your fault. Almost all supervisors and managers in the United States today got their jobs by executive fiat. Probably, they promoted you because you excelled at your previous job. You were a top-performing salesperson, so they made you the sales manager. You were an accomplished and effective customer service rep so they made you the team leader. But they probably offered little or no training for your first supervisory job, as if they expected you to learn managerial skills via osmosis or divine inspiration.

Corporations have seldom invested enough in training managers and supervisors; in recent years they have invested next to nothing. The results are that millions of bosses grope in the dark, trying to do their jobs as best they can. Unfortunately, because they are not trained to be managers, their staff lose self-esteem, job satisfaction, and their health and well-being. Their companies suffer poor productivity and work quality, dissatisfied customers, high turnover, and workplace conflict that cost the organizations billions.

Management is hard work. It taxes us mentally and physically. That is why it pays more. That is why it accords you greater prestige in your community and greater status within your company. If you are in middle management, you are pulled in several directions. You have the needs of your employees, the demands of your management, and competition from your peers to deal with. You may feel overtaxed.

On the other hand, the title of manager and the perks that go with it imply that your primary focus must be on the productivity and the morale of the people who work for you.

How to Be a Better Boss

I cannot tell you, in one chapter, everything you need to know. Leadership and managerial skills are subjects that fill many books, but the following section offers some important advice to set you on the right path.

Think of Your Employees as a Resource

Employees are a source of energy and creativity to further the company's goals, and it's up to you to mobilize them. They are not a cost center that needs to be controlled or a difficulty that needs to be dealt with. If you see them as an asset, not a liability, your thought processes will automatically draw you to the positive.

Hone Your Leadership Skills

- Make sure your employees know exactly what is expected of them and have everything they need to get the job done, including training, technology, budget, authority, information, and time.
- Tell them how their performance will be measured. To the extent that you can influence such decisions, make sure they are rewarded for their accomplishments.
- Be sure they understand how their work fits into the overall goals of the organization.
- Tell your people the truth about what's going on in the company, events and decisions that might affect their lives.
- Never keep them in the dark about their career prospects.
- Be supportive. Your job is to help them to achieve excellence and to feel good about achieving it. This will draw their motivation to the tasks at hand.

Always Have the Person Who Makes a Mistake Correct It

Closing the circle of information in this way will make your operation more efficient and give your people the dignity of learning to achieve their goals. Do this in a supportive way. Berating or abusing employees who make mistakes only causes them to make more. When workers perform poorly, they need a chance to learn to succeed. Making them feel bad, ashamed of their work, or resentful of your authority will accomplish nothing. Show them, in an encouraging way, how to do it right. If you have a person who never gets it, put him in a different job if he is willing but incapable, or dismiss her if she is capable but unwilling to do it right. People who refuse to do their jobs are not doing themselves, your other employees, or the organization any good. What they need is to go find a job they really want to do.

Bolster Your Own Confidence

Keep your ego out of the way. If it makes you feel powerful to make them cower, you need help with your own self-image. Maybe the role you fill feels like a suit that doesn't fit. You can and must get comfortable with what you are doing. Get training. Get advice. Find the style of interacting with them that works for the group—not just what feels good to you, but what energizes them.

Show Your Enthusiasm

If you have no enthusiasm for your work, how can you inspire those who work for you? If you've got it, flaunt it. If you don't have it, get it or get another job. How could a coach who hated basketball ever coach a winning team?

Don't Blame Your Boss

Regardless of what a crazy, dim, or misguided monster he is, blaming your boss for your failures as a manager sends the wrong message to your staff. Even if you have legitimate beefs, don't air them in front of your employees. If your boss insists that you do things that are counterproductive, find the courage to resist. Use the techniques discussed in this book to manage your boss so that you can in turn manage your people well. Feeling sorry for yourself and badmouthing your manager will make you appear weak and ineffectual. These traits will score no points with those above or below you on the organization chart.

Be Yourself

Do not try to adopt a special managerial personality. Reject management advice that tells you what kind of person you have to be to be a successful manager. Your best approach is to be natural and authentic. If you are annoyed but try to act as if nothing is bothering you, the dishonesty of your message will show through. You will confuse your employees. They will not know what you want them to do or, worse yet, whether they can trust what you are saying. They will end up guessing. And they will guess wrong. On the other hand, you must not express that annoyance in a destructive way. Find a way to say what is wrong that is direct and clear without being mean.

If your personality does not lend itself to managing comfortably, why are you in this job? If you do not have what it takes to lead, you will not succeed. Your increased pay and status will be short lived and too dearly bought. Find another way to contribute. If you have personal problems that interfere with your managing well, find a way to solve them or you will never enjoy your job, and neither will anyone who reports to you.

Capitalize on Your Strengths

A manager's time is fragmented. You may have to work at a frantic pace. This may cause you not to pay enough attention to your own management skills. Take the time to figure out which of your managerial practices pay off and which do not. Keep a log of your management actions and how they pan out. Do this for a month or two and see which techniques work for you. Drop the failing behaviors from your repertoire.

Set an Example

Those who work for you will model their managerial behavior after yours. You can have the pleasure of shaping the behaviors of a whole generation of managers under you. If they, you, and the organization are going to prosper, you all have to use management techniques that pay off and that last.

Create a Sense of Group Identity and Cohesiveness

You will all enjoy your jobs, come to work brimming with motivation, and produce more and better work if you feel connected as a team. Lots of things can help you create this. Here is an easy one. Gather the group together at the beginning of every week, go over the work schedules and issues to be faced; get everyone to participate in the plan. Use this time also to explain how what they are doing fits into the organization's goals, to respond to their problems, and to discuss how to resolve them as a group. But keep this brief and productive. We are *not* talking about gripe sessions or group therapy here. This is a business meeting, where you listen to their needs. The discussion should produce an action plan for the team. This should take a half hour or so.

It is particularly important in this atmosphere to get your staff to find ways to support one another's work. If Claudia is overloaded, find out if Steve or Jeanette has extra time to spare to help her out. That sort of thing promotes collaboration and cooperation. Give your employees a sense of belonging and participation and they will respond with commitment. Human beings need to feel they are members of the tribe. Their job satisfaction will soar if they understand that, as a cohesive group, they are contributing to a result you all believe in.

Control the Work, Not the People

Remember, your job is to get the work done, not to be a puppeteer who dictates everyone's precise actions. Your people will do their jobs willingly if they see their needs as people satisfied in the doing. Find out what they want from their jobs and arrange for them to get as much of it as you can. In such circumstances, they will do more than you have the nerve to demand. Allow them to be themselves and bring out the best in them. Do not try to impose personality or character traits on them. It will not work any better with them than it does when your boss tries to do that with you.

Stay Motivated

Above all, keep yourself motivated. Mangers in management development programs often complain that their own bosses do not practice the principles of good management. Students of management know they are supposed to follow advice like that given above, but they, too, want to be treated well by their supervisors. They want their managers to motivate them. It does not always happen.

Given that you cannot dictate to your boss, you may have to practice do-it-yourself motivation. If you allow your manager to take your motivation away from you, it is you who will have been robbed. You can point to your boss as the cause. You may even be able to tell the people who work for you that your hands are tied. But you are going to have to be the cure.

It's this simple: You are in charge of your life.

GEORGE'S STORY

George Rivera learned this from one well-placed sentence. He was working as a staff group head in the chairman's office of a packaged goods company. It was a prestigious job, but George felt like the head butler since he considered many of his assignments trivial—arranging luncheons, supervising the scheduling of the corporate jet. He did his work enthusiastically at first, hoping that success in the easy projects would lead to more rewarding assignments. When his hopes did not pan out, he decided to ask his boss, the company's administrative vice president, how he could get into a job more central to what the company did. That talk got him exactly nowhere. The VP offered little more than vague reasons, alluded to George's personality and the realism of his expectations. Nothing improved.

For a month or so after that meeting, George ran on automatic pilot, doing the best job he could. Then, the discouragement started to set in. He felt he had nothing to look forward to in his work future. That depressed him. He knew that his staff of four felt his discouragement, and he found it nearly impossible to imbue them with a sense of excitement when he discussed their projects with them. He was afraid his negativity would soon pervade his entire staff.

He thought about quitting, but he could not bring himself to do it. He justified staying by citing the difficulties of getting another job. He told himself he should feel lucky to have the position he had. Lots of his friends envied the glamour of it. He might not command the same salary if he had to start over somewhere else. He had to think of the mortgage payment, his kids' education. So he stayed, even as he felt more and more trapped and became more and more dejected about his work.

One day Earl, the pilot of the corporate jet, walked by and saw George looking sad. Earl walked into George's office and sat down. "You look awful, George," he said. "What is wrong?"

"I feel like a bird in a cage," George answered.

Earl faced George squarely and said, "The door is open" and walked out. George sat there a few more minutes and went on with his work. Later on, though, he would trace the beginning of changes in his life to that one sentence of Earl's. Those four words opened a peephole to a better future and rescued George from his own refusal to deal with what was happening to him. They helped George realize that he made his own choices and, to that extent, determined his own future. He decided to stop being his own victim. In the end, George found a job that challenged him. He took a temporary cut in pay to do it, but with his increased energy and enthusiasm, he soon made up for it by moving up the ladder in his new job. Now his life is better financially and psychologically than it ever would have been if he had stayed in his old job and let his motivation die.

You're in Charge

Free will is a scary concept. It means you are in charge of your own motivation, in the driver's seat when it comes to your career. And it means you set your own destination and choose your own route.

The choice of what to want and what to avoid is yours. If you are ambitious, fine. If you do not feel like joining the corporate rat race, that is fine, too. Do not allow other people or the prevailing culture to tell you that the fast lane is where you must be. It is hard enough to marshal the energy to reach your own goals. How can you possibly find the motivation to strive for career goals set for you by others? In making career choices, follow the heat and the light. Be sensible, but move toward what attracts you most. Strong feelings are often clues about needs buried deep within us. By following them, you may tap energy and ambition you did not know were there. If you deny your feelings, you may be denying an underlying truth about yourself that will haunt you and cause you to fail.

Stay Flexible

If you bend, you will not break. Remember, no matter how carefully you plan your career, no matter how confident you are, no matter how much energy you put into your work, life is going to give you some surprises. This is a mystery story we are all living, and what makes it interesting is that we do not know how it will turn out. Set your goals, but leave some room for the unexpected.

Remember, too, that if you do not achieve your objective in one area, you will have other opportunities. The days of single career paths are over. Experts say that today's workers will have as many as five careers. Change and risk and growth are bound to be part of your work life and that of your employees.

Be a Leader

If you can keep your motivation going, you will have a chance of helping your staff stay energized. Keeping them focused and motivated should be the guiding principle of all your activities as a manager. In other words, be a leader, not just a manager. What is the difference? Managers, as we have said, are made by executive fiat. Managers answer to their bosses. Leaders answer to their followers. Your people will follow you if they think you are leading them to success, if you are for them and support them, help them grow, give them a sense of belonging, participation, and accomplishment.

Lao Tzu, the ancient Chinese sage, put it succinctly:

That leader is best
Whose people say,
When the job is done,
We did it ourselves.

APPENDIX A

GOALS

Use this space to set your goals.

- *Make your objectives realistic.* Your goal should be aimed at making your work life more satisfying and successful and less stressful, to put your career on a positive track.
- *Do not set goals that involve changing the boss's personality.* Attempts to change the boss's behavior toward you are fair goals, but stay reasonable in your expectations of success.
- *Be specific.* A goal that says "To make progress" is worse than no goal at all. A proper goal is one that has a clear indication of when it is achieved. "To visit San Francisco" is a clear goal. You will know when you get there that you have achieved it.

MONSTER BOSS

APPENDIX B

EXIT STRATEGY

Sources of Job Information

Web sites that list jobs:

Resume services:

Contact information for people who can help:

INDEX